"Li Zhang's book shines modern industrial food production practices and ecological destruction are distorting nature and leading to the emergence of new zoonotic infectious diseases like SARS, COVID-19, and virulent influenzas."

—Joan Kaufman, Harvard Medical School

"Zhang rigorously combines science and politics to show that this pandemic should not be blamed on China, but rather on the structural conditions of global capitalism, modernization, and uncritical scientism worldwide. This is a major and unique contribution."

—Sun Jin, Beijing Normal University

"In a time of profound confusion and escalating misreporting and disinformation, Li Zhang's new book is a rare oasis of lucid, serious discussion of China's predicament in and response to the COVID-19 pandemic."

—Christos Lynteris, University of St. Andrews

"This book offers an absorbing account of the key events surrounding COVID-19 as they continue to unfold across the world. A timely reminder that as new viruses emerge, they also reproduce and sharpen existing unevenness in our inextricably entangled world."

—Mei Zhan, University of California, Irvine

"As part of an alternative solution to future pandemic risks, Zhang calls for a new paradigm in food production that is diametrically different from the current capitalist mode of production. This is a must-read for policy makers and for all who are concerned with public health, environmental protection, and food production."

—Peter J. Li, University of Houston-Downtown

THE ORIGINS OF COVID-19

China and Global Capitalism

LI ZHANG

stanford briefs
An Imprint of Stanford University Press
Stanford, California

Stanford University Press
Stanford, California

Printed in the United States of America on acid-free, archival-quality
paper

Library of Congress Cataloging-in-Publication Data

Names: Zhang, Li (Assistant professor), author.
Title: The origins of COVID-19 : China and global capitalism / Li
    Zhang.
Description: Stanford, California : Stanford Briefs, an imprint of
    Stanford University Press, 2021. | Includes bibliographical
    references. |
Identifiers: LCCN 2021020375 (print) | LCCN 2021020376 (ebook) |
    ISBN 9781503630178 (paperback) | ISBN 9781503630185 (ebook)
Subjects: LCSH: COVID-19 (Disease)—China. | COVID-19
    (Disease)—Government policy—China. | COVID-19 Pandemic,
    2020—-China. | Capitalism—Health aspects—China.
Classification: LCC RA644.C67 Z429 2021 (print) | LCC RA644.
    C67 (ebook) | DDC 362.1962/41400951—dc23
LC record available at https://lccn.loc.gov/2021020375
LC ebook record available at https://lccn.loc.gov/2021020376

Cover design: Kevin Barrett Kane
Cover image: Afif Kusuma

Typeset by Classic Typography in 11/15 Adobe Garamond

DEDICATED TO VENTURO ZHANG OLIVEIRA
AND ALL OTHERS WHO LOST THEIR LIVES AND
LOVED ONES DURING THE COVID-19 PANDEMIC.

. . . we might try to explain the phenomenon of the plague, but, above all, should learn what it had to teach us.

—Albert Camus, *The Plague*

CONTENTS

THE ORIGINS OF COVID·19

1 PRELUDE

At first, a few cases of pneumonia of unknown origin began to appear in a fast-growing industrial city in China. The earliest cluster of cases was traced to a wet market that sold wild animals, traditional delicacies whose demand flourished with the new consumerism that has engulfed China since its market-oriented reforms. Soon, local hospitals were becoming swamped with new patients, and healthcare workers themselves began to fall ill. Unable to cure or contain the mysterious new disease, hospitals became the center of new outbreaks. The Chinese government at first tried to censor reports about the new disease, suppressing journalists and healthcare workers who dared blow the whistle. But China's fast urbanization and new infrastructures facilitated the eruption of the emergent disease into a national epidemic, and the government could no longer hide that something was horribly wrong. To make things worse, in the couple of months since it emerged the previous

November, the infection began to spread beyond China's borders. That an avian or swine flu pandemic might originate in China, where rapid urbanization intersects with a boom in industrial chicken and pig farms, was already well known.[1] But scientists around the world were astonished to discover this disease resulted not from influenza, but from a novel *coronavirus* instead. Recognizing the risk of an impending pandemic, the Chinese government shifted radically from hesitation and denials to forceful quarantines, strict surveillance of whole populations, and massive deployment of biomedical staff and resources. A new specialized hospital was built in a matter of days. Within a few months, the epidemic was successfully contained in China. The year was 2003, and the new disease was named for its symptoms, severe acute respiratory syndrome—SARS.[2]

This story resonates eerily with the present. A novel strain of coronavirus appeared again sometime in 2019, and within weeks a cluster of patients began to be admitted to hospitals in the metropolis of Wuhan with severe pneumonia, many of them linked to the Huanan Seafood Wholesale Market.[3] With unprecedented speed, the outbreak in Wuhan became epidemic across China, and then pandemic around the world, affecting millions on every continent and bringing the global economy to its knees. This new disease, COVID-19, has become a world historical force reshaping the intertwined futures of China and global capitalism.

The origins of COVID-19 and the manner in which various governments controlled (or failed to control) the epidemic has been highly politicized. Public debate in the West focuses on China's supposedly "backward" cultural practices of consuming wild animals and the perceived problem of authoritarianism suppressing information until it was too late to prevent the local outbreak from becoming a global pandemic. Chinese public debate also blamed wet markets at first, then shifted focus to frozen food imports that might implicate other countries in the origins of COVID-19. Both Chinese and Western discourses converge in a narrative that emphasizes the biomedical capacity of the Chinese government to successfully contain the disease (e.g., quickly building field hospitals, enforcing quarantines, etc.). The goal of this book is to shift debate away from narrow cultural, political, or biomedical frameworks, emphasizing that we must understand the origins of emerging diseases with pandemic potential (such as SARS and COVID-19) in much more complex and structural entanglements of state-making, science and technology, and global capitalism. In other words, the purpose is to guide a global debate toward the most pertinent questions we need to ask to not simply explain the phenomenon of COVID-19, but also to understand how we may be able to prevent the continued emergence of pandemic diseases.

Nothing like this current crisis has been seen in a century. Yet the emergence of SARS in 2002 and its relatively limited spread from China to other countries in Asia, North America, Europe, and beyond during 2003 were undeniably a prelude. Tracing the main characteristics of the SARS outbreak in China—examining why it originated there, how the Chinese government and society responded to the crisis, and in what ways biomedical science, state-making, and global capitalism became entangled by these events—lays the foundation for the book's subsequent analysis of the novel coronavirus pandemic we are now facing. The "lessons learned" from the SARS outbreak, including advancements in virology, epidemiology, public health governance, and biomedical science, evidently failed to prevent the emergence of another novel coronavirus.

Of course, the scale of the SARS outbreak and the COVID-19 pandemic are radically distinct. Official World Health Organization (WHO) figures place the number of cases of SARS in mainland China at 5,327 and the number of deaths at 349,[4] while China effectively contained the COVID-19 epidemic within the country with about 84,000 confirmed cases and about 4,600 deaths by May 2020.[5] However, the much more glaring contrast lies in the fact that SARS spread only to another twenty-nine countries, infecting a total of 8,096 people and causing the deaths of about 811 worldwide. COVID-19, on the other hand, has spread to every country in the world, infecting 173 million people and causing about 3.8 million deaths by June 2021. Unfortunately, despite the record development of vaccines, COVID-19 will continue to infect millions and kill countless more, especially as it spreads further among the poorest and most vulnerable in the Global South and becomes endemic. But it is also notable that Europe and the US each confirmed over a million cases of COVID-19 within three months of their first cases of the epidemic, and the number of deaths surpassed tens of thousands; these wealthy regions have faced even larger surges since then. This is, thus, in part a story about the Chinese government's unparalleled command over biomedical resources and digital surveillance, capacity for mass mobilization of the population, state control of the economy, and the paradoxical nature of this state power as instrument of national development in the era of global capitalism.

The hallmarks of modernity and economic development in China, celebrated as the instruments used by the state to successfully control the epidemic, are at the root of this and other emerging diseases with pandemic potential. Consequently, any critical study of the origins of the COVID-19 pandemic cannot limit itself to biomedical examinations abstracted from politics and place (as much of the scientific literature tends to do), nor to a critique of China's culture and state (as much of the popular literature tends to do), but must combine them and extend beyond into an analysis of the condition of global capitalist modernity in which China is embedded.

Scholars like Rob Wallace and Mike Davis have shown that the mounting risk of catastrophic influenza pandemics results from the specific political ecologies of capitalist agribusiness that have emerged in recent decades and coalesced above all in southern China.[6] "This new age of plagues, like previous pandemic epochs, is directly the result of economic globalization," explains Davis.[7] "Permanent bio-protection against new plagues, accordingly, would require more than vaccines. It would need the suppression of these 'structures of disease emergence' through revolutionary reforms in agriculture and urban living that no large capitalist or state-capitalist country would ever willingly undertake."[8] I join Davis in calling for the replacement of capitalist approaches with alternative models for responding to all such plagues. But considering how Donald Trump's anti-science zealotry shaped the catastrophe, Davis goes on to conclude that these must be models that "put science in command."[9] Keeping China at the center of my analysis, however, also requires problematizing the way biomedical science and practice have become the hegemonic framework through which we understand pandemics, and through which governments, individuals, and corporations react to them. In other words, understanding the origins of COVID-19, and how the Chinese state and society addressed its emergence, requires a critique that delves deeper than global capitalism alone and into the heart of discourses about modernization, development, environmental degradation, and the prospects for global health and sustainability in the new century.

After all, virology, epidemiology, public health governance, and other biomedical sciences are not a politically neutral terrain upon which government officials and the masses can find the supposedly objective truth about diseases like influenza, SARS, and COVID-19, and thus serve unambiguously as guides for how to prevent, mitigate, and respond to such emerging diseases. These diseases can indeed be examined through virology, epidemiology, and clinical characteristics, and responses to them certainly must involve biomedical interventions like vaccines, pharmaceuticals, expanded hospital networks, and strengthened apparatuses of public health surveillance and control. Yet limiting our understanding of emerging diseases to the biomedical conceals the structural conditions of global capitalism that give rise to emerging diseases in the first place and promotes biomedical responses that cannot contain their emergence, but may even increase the risk of viruses "spilling over" from animals to humans, and aggravate the conditions that propel these outbreaks into catastrophic pandemics. Ultimately, therefore, "new ways of thinking about basic biology, evolution, and scientific practice are in order."[10]

This is especially the case in China, where the preeminence of modern science and technology is unparalleled.[11] Even during the most radical and euphoric periods of Mao's anti-capitalist revolution, for example, the authority of scientists and scientific institutions were politically and ideologically challenged, but rather than the anti-science zealotry we witness presently among conservatives in the US, there was instead a sincere effort to democratize science and incorporate the practical needs and experiential knowledge of the masses into a modernist project that could serve the interests of the masses and their socialist nation-state in the making.[12] With Deng Xiaoping's model of development, this Maoist transformation of science was abandoned, even as the party and government leadership swelled with scientists and engineers, transforming reform-era

China into a "virtual technocracy."[13] Since then, Chinese government and society have pursued science and technology with such fervor and optimism, seeing this as "the essential key to making China globally competitive and addressing the nation's confounding domestic problems," that such "scientism" is virtually "immune to social critique."[14] And yet, contemporary China harbors such a powerful convergence of strong state management and rampant capitalist expansion that scientific practice and technological development are hampered, on the one hand, by bureaucratic demands to produce "correct" data that aligns with policy goals even if it does not conform with reality and, on the other hand, by market imperatives that lead to "science that is fragmentary at best and practically ineffective or even harmful at worst."[15] The roots of the current pandemic in outbreaks of novel coronavirus diseases in China, and the manner in which the Chinese state and society have responded to these events through state and market logics, expose this entanglement of state-making and global capitalism through modern science and technology.

Ultimately, bringing this entanglement into focus prefigures a debate about the lessons to be learned from the current pandemic, particularly whether the world should blame China and be wary of what it unleashes into the world, or celebrate and emulate its successful efforts to contain the epidemic and reignite its massive economy through strong state control. And revealing this entanglement also serves as a warning that the recovery of a capitalist economy in China and its political responses to the current crisis reinforce the conditions for infectious diseases with pandemic potential to emerge again and again, and yet this is not about China itself, but about the conditions of global capitalism in which China is embedded.

The next chapter turns to the COVID-19 outbreak that emerged in Wuhan during late 2019 and the failure of the local government to trigger the institutional alarms that were created in the aftermath of SARS. The subsequent chapters trace various stages of the epidemic—the uncertainty among government, scientific, and corporate actors in efforts to contain and control the burgeoning COVID-19 epidemic during January 2020; the surge of the disease across China and into a global pandemic during February and March; and the declaration of victory and the reopening of Wuhan in April. The final chapter describes the persistence of the disease through the end of 2020, analyzes the global capitalist competition and geopolitical tensions exacerbated by the pandemic, and critiques the persistence of the political, cultural, and ecological factors that are intended to drive economic "recovery" but may reinforce the risk of future pandemics. Finally, the epilogue looks back to debates about the origins of COVID-19 and forward to the development of vaccines, underscoring the argument that public debate and research should extend beyond biomedical concerns and the particularities of China to focus on the structural conditions of global capitalism.

But first, a brief note on methodology. I drew upon official reports and statements from various levels of the Chinese government and the WHO; an in-depth engagement with scholarly publications in the fields of biology, virology, epidemiology, medicine, and public health (including important but underinvestigated Chinese-language publications); and also history and social sciences, including anthropology, sociology, political science, geography, economics, and interdisciplinary fields such as environmental, agrarian, development, and global studies. I also extensively examined Chinese and international journalistic and social media materials—including materials that I archived before they were removed or altered. The approach is to formulate a transdisciplinary synthesis that can reframe questions and analysis interlinking various fields.

ZOONOSIS

There are competing narratives about the emergence of diseases like SARS and COVID-19 in China. One of the most common is that China's "uncivilized," "exotic," "premodern" culture is responsible for their origins. After all, once virologists identified the genomic sequence of the novel coronaviruses that cause SARS (SARS-CoV) and COVID-19 (SARS-CoV-2), an international scientific consensus developed that these viruses emerged from strains endemic among bats, which likely jumped through another wild animal species and mutated in a way that enables the virus to infect humans. In other words, the emergence of these diseases is due to *zoonosis*, the spill-over of a pathogen from an animal species into humans.

In the case of SARS, the outbreak was traced back to a spillover from masked palm civets, which were traded in the wet markets of Guangdong province, where the outbreak started, and a few years later to bats as the original and natural reservoir of the SARS coronavirus.[16] In the case of the 2012 outbreak of a similar coronavirus disease originating in the Middle East (hence named the Middle East respiratory syndrome—MERS), the outbreak was traced to camels or goats as the likely intermediaries between bats and humans.[17] In the case of COVID-19, the specific animal species through which the novel coronavirus likely infected humans remains unclear, but it appears evident the virus originated in bats as well.[18] Thus, a video of a Chinese travel blogger eating bat soup on a Pacific island went viral during the early days of the pandemic, and racist commentary in international media misled the public to believe that COVID-19 may have emerged due to Chinese people's "exotic" or even "revolting" dietary habits.[19] Such feelings were even widespread among Chinese people themselves. Although this "bat soup hypothesis" was immediately debunked, this narrative retains power because the Huanan wet market clusters most of the earliest known cases of this outbreak in Wuhan, enabling epidemiologists to hypothesize COVID-19 may be traceable to the farming or trafficking of wildlife for traditional Chinese medicine (TCM), fashion, and prized exotic meals, such as pangolins, minks, bamboo rats, or other animals susceptible to coronavirus strains quite similar to SARS-CoV-2.[20]

But culture alone cannot account for spillover events, which are conditioned by political and ecological transformations that attach China intimately to global capitalism. Wild animal consumption has a long history in China, especially in southern provinces like Guangdong. Yet consumption only increased recently with the rising prevalence of chronic diseases, driving consumerist desire for "natural" foods, supposedly untainted by the toxic chemicals used in the modern farming and livestock industry. This results in further commodification of TCM.[21] Likewise, China's postsocialist transformation rests on massive rural-urban migration, the lifeblood of rapid industrialization, but also a vector that connects remote villages where humans might come into contact with wild animals to major urban centers where an outbreak has far greater epidemic potential.

All of these factors were already in place by the late 1990s, especially in Guangdong province where the earliest establishment of China's export-oriented industrialization left the environment highly polluted and migrant-worker populations tightly concentrated in fast-growing cities. Moreover, rising incomes fueled consumerism for TCMs that were intended to protect individuals from precisely the sorts of diseases that emerge and spread most rapidly in such places and conditions. It is no simple irony, therefore, that the civets through which the SARS coronavirus probably spilled over into humans are consumed because of their alleged properties to improve the immune system.[22] Yet even though the identification of civets and other wild animals as the most likely vector for the spillover of SARS into the human population led to a crackdown on unregulated wet markets and a temporary ban on sale of civets, public policy quickly shifted from the prevention of zoonosis toward strengthening public health surveillance and the development of pharmaceutical treatments and vaccines.[23]

After all, focus on zoonosis prevention would require investigating the increasingly important social practice of gift-exchange among elites that includes wild animals as part of lavish meals, traditional medicines, and luxury fashion items. "The majority of the people in China do not eat wildlife animals," explains Peter Li. "Those people who consume these wildlife animals are the rich and the powerful—a small minority."[24] Moreover, cracking down on this practice also entails halting an increasingly profitable new business sector in wildlife trade, even as wet markets in southern China become the visual embodiment of a pandemic ground zero.[25] According to researchers from the Chinese Academy of Forestry, China has successfully established captive breeding populations for over 230 wildlife species. By 2006, there were already over 19,000 farms raising wildlife commercially, and their products were processed by about 3,166 companies. Despite the recognition that SARS spread to humans most likely through farmed civets, the sector has continued to experience "unprecedented growth."[26] According to the most extensive and systematic report on China's wildlife industry, produced by the Chinese Academy of Engineering, the sector in 2016 already included over 14 million people working across wild animal breeding, wildlife product processing, trading, and consumption, and related tourism, producing a collective output of 520 billion yuan (about $78 billion USD).[27]

Ultimately, the Chinese government's approach to wildlife consumption has been to increasingly regulate it, and thus even promote it, as a new commercial, industrial, and revenue-generating sector of the economy. The main policy proposal of the Chinese Academy of Engineering's report on the wildlife industry, for example, is a call to increasingly "domesticate" wild animals through livestock breeding, relying on higher technology and "scientific" livestock management techniques to scale-up and industrialize production and processing for increased commercialization.[28] Yet this state, scientific, and capitalist strategy of "conservation through utilization" actually increases production and consumption of wildlife products and the animal-human interface through which novel diseases may spill over.[29] For example, while thousands of civets were culled in 2004 and their sale and consumption were temporarily restricted again in 2006 (when their role in the SARS outbreak was confirmed), by 2016 over 50,000 civets were raised and sold within China for an estimated 50 million yuan ($7.5 million USD).[30] A similarly dizzying number and variety of insects, wild birds, snakes, turtles, frogs, lizards, crocodiles, bamboo rats, raccoons, badgers, ferrets, minks, foxes, pangolins, monkeys, deer, boars, and even bears are all raised, slaughtered, processed, and commercialized for fashion, food, cosmetic, and medicinal products of various sorts, and sometimes for use as pets or in laboratory research, not only in China but also for international trade.[31]

Rather than confronting directly the structural political, economic, and ecological conditions that expand the human-wildlife interface in ways that increase the risk of new spillover events, China's state and society responded to the SARS outbreak with modernist state-making efforts to professionalize public health and biomedical science (including TCM) as the key strategy to address the growing risk of pandemic diseases in China.[32] This involved an approach to the problem of zoonosis that prioritizes invasive surveillance and experimentation on pathogens. And across the board, the interests of policy makers, scientists, and business leaders in China became increasingly entangled with the institutional frameworks and capitalist imperatives of international partners, ranging from the expansion of Chinese medical aid in the Global South to partnerships with virologists and investors from universities and pharmaceutical companies from the Global North.

In 2005, for example, the confirmation that SARS originated from bats triggered a swell of interest and funding for research on bats and coronaviruses, and Chinese scientists integrated global networks researching such animal vector-borne diseases (e.g., EcoHealth Alliance and the

Global Virome Project). [33] According to a propaganda video coproduced by the China Association of Science and Technology, China Academy of Sciences (CAS), China Central Television (CCTV), and the Wuhan Municipal Center for Disease Control and Prevention (Wuhan CDC), "nearly 2,000 types of viruses have been discovered by Chinese CDC authorities" between 2007 and 2019, while "only 2,284 types of viruses had been discovered worldwide over the 200 years prior to China's discovery."[34] In the process of rapidly expanding research on animal vector-borne diseases, however, some of the leading scholars and practitioners of virus sample collection and classification in Wuhan would become entangled in debates about the origins of the current coronavirus pandemic itself.

Tian Junhua is one of these practitioners. As associate chief technician at the Department of Disinfection and Pest Control of the Wuhan CDC, he became a minor celebrity in his field, interviewed in several news articles and the video mentioned above.[35] That video shows Tian and his team venturing into bat-infested caves to study them. Tian narrates: "In the past 10-plus years, we have visited every corner in Hubei province. We explored dozens of undeveloped caves, and studied more than 300 types of virus vectors."[36] Then he states the risks associated with this work: "If we keep our skin bare, we can easily get contact with the feces of bats which contaminate everything. So it is highly risky here . . . I can feel the fear, fear of infections . . . because when you find the viruses, you are also most easily exposed to the viruses."[37]

Indeed, as Tian reported elsewhere, in some of these excursions he was accidentally exposed to bat urine and possible infections and had to quarantine himself afterward as a precaution.[38] So why would he expose himself to such risk of infection? Tian argues, "Only when we find more vectors can we lay a firm foundation for making vaccines. This is our mission."[39] Yet just a few moments later in the same video, Tian also admits that "humans need not only the vaccines, but also protection from nature."[40] There is evidently a tension, therefore, between the practice of venturing into remote areas to scour bats for virus samples that might be useful for research and the need to minimize the human-wildlife interface through which spillovers occur in the first place.

This tension is not limited to Tian's work, but is rather a characteristic of modern virology and biomedical science in general. The research conducted by Shi Zhengli, for example, one of the most famous virologists in China, features this tension even more prominently. In 2000, she obtained her PhD in virology from the Montpellier University in France and together with other scholars, led efforts to sample thousands of bats throughout China, isolating over 300 coronavirus genetic sequences from them.[41] Much of this work was done in collaboration with researchers in the US, Australia, and France, including government laboratories that partnered with the CAS to expand the Wuhan Institute of Virology's (WIV) biosecurity capacity to the highest biosafety level (BSL-4). When the WIV inaugurated its BSL-4 laboratory in

January 2018, Wuhan was the first Chinese city to host such an advanced scientific enterprise. This research led Shi and her colleagues to conclude: "The constant spill-over of viruses from natural hosts to humans and other animals is largely *due to human activities*, including modern agricultural practices and urbanization. Therefore, the most effective way to prevent viral zoonosis is to *maintain the barriers between natural reservoirs and human society*."[42]

Yet in the process of undertaking their own scientific investigations, these researchers have literally dug deeper into the bowels of bats and their caves than ever before in human history and brought samples of their viruses into densely populated and globally interconnected cities like Wuhan, albeit protected by world-class apparatuses of biosecurity. Shi justifies this research practice similarly to Tian, arguing that "bat-borne coronaviruses will cause more outbreaks, [so] we must find them before they find us"[43] and that "the purpose of the search for the origin of a virus is to prevent the recurrence of similar outbreaks which will harm human society, and in this way, we can respond more effectively when an outbreak happens."[44]

Indeed, the advancements in research undertaken on bat coronaviruses between the SARS outbreak and the emergence of COVID-19 enabled scientists to genetically identify the virus causing these diseases and respond with diagnostic tests and vaccines far more rapidly. After the first case of SARS was publicly identified as a disease of unknown origin in Guangdong, it took three months for scientists in Hong Kong to isolate the SARS-CoV virus and five months to develop a rapid diagnostic test to detect it, which could thus improve diagnosis, contact tracing, and individually targeted quarantines.[45] By that point, however, the spread of the new disease had already effectively halted within China due to a nationwide mobilization that paused all social gatherings and placed entire villages, neighborhoods, and even whole cities effectively under lockdown.[46] By contrast, after cases of severe pneumonia of an unknown origin began to be clinically identified in Wuhan during December 2019, it took less than a month for scientists in China to isolate the virus, and rapid tests for the novel coronavirus were developed just a few days later in January 2020.[47] This prompt capacity for testing and tracing the contacts of infected individuals enabled China and a few other countries to contain the COVID-19 epidemic in its early stages, and this has been especially important because COVID-19 can spread much more easily than SARS or MERS, including even by asymptomatic carriers. Moreover, the SARS and MERS outbreaks encouraged the development of coronavirus vaccines, and even though none was completed before 2020, that research served as the foundation for the record-speed development of COVID-19 vaccines.

But based upon this rationale, Shi and various collaborators in the US and Switzerland were going much further than identifying viruses and developing diagnostic tests and vaccines. They have conducted "gain-of-function" experiments on SARS and SARS-like viruses, which enhances the viruses to see whether and how their virulence increases in human cells.[48] These experiments seek to better understand the way viruses attack the human body, but the associated risks of strengthening deadly viruses even further—or even to enable the transformation of viruses into biological weapons—has caused widespread condemnation of such research practices. In 2014 the US government even imposed a moratorium on "gain-of-function" experiments such as the ones Shi and her partners were conducting, cutting their funds from the National Institute of Health.[49] After all, the risk of a research-related incident triggering an outbreak is very low but real nonetheless.

In 2014, the US Food and Drug Administration found six vials of smallpox accidentally abandoned in an insecure storage room.[50] That same year, the US Center for Disease Control and Prevention (CDC) accidentally sent viable anthrax spores to three insecure labs, possibly exposing researchers to the deadly bacteria.[51] Then in 2015, the Pentagon accidentally shipped live anthrax to nine states and even to South Korea.[52] Thankfully, those accidents did not cause any deaths. Yet there were at least 1,141 instances of "laboratory acquired infections" reported worldwide between 1979 and 2005, some of which have resulted in deaths.[53] This is not to promote a "lab leak" hypothesis for COVID-19, but rather to call for further discussion of the benefits *and risks* of mass collection and manipulation of pathogens around the world, such as through the Global Virome Project and the work of the

EcoHealth Alliance. Similarly, the national and international developments in institutional modernization for biosecurity, reporting on infectious disease outbreaks, public health preparedness, epidemic control, and infectious disease treatment also require careful examination.

MODERNIZATION

The SARS epidemic consolidated an approach to public health that prioritizes surveillance of the population and expansion of the state and biomedical apparatuses for disease treatment and control, a form of capitalist expansion and state-making that sets goals and priorities in ways that might not effectively eliminate the threat of novel diseases, but rather render them *governable* and even *profitable* to handle.[54] Yet this conjunction of state and market logics did not unfold because China was an outlier to global capitalism and international institutions of public health; rather it occurred precisely in the way they came together in the aftermath of the SARS crisis.

The outbreak of SARS may have been quite small compared to the anticipated avian flu pandemic considered to be an imminent threat emanating from southern China since the late 1990s, or compared to the present COVID-19 pandemic, but it dramatically shaped the trajectory of both China and global public health institutions. The WHO had just established the first Global Outbreak Alert and Response Network (GOARN) in 2000, interconnecting various surveillance systems that already existed among certain UN and government agencies, scientific institutions, and nongovernmental organizations (NGOs) around the world. The SARS outbreak was the first opportunity for the GOARN to come into action. After all, the Chinese government was initially reluctant to provide public information about the SARS outbreak in Guangdong province, denied it was suspected to be a novel infectious disease (insisting instead it was merely chlamydia), and suppressed reports that it appeared to be a respiratory disease with pandemic potential. But the GOARN was able to gather enough biomedical data from nongovernment sources to indicate that an unknown epidemic was rapidly spreading in China. According to the leader of this WHO response, "This rapid reaction was critical to the containment of the epidemic by July 2003, although he also acknowledged the good fortune that SARS turned out not to be as easily transmissible as initially feared."[55] Still, the WHO learned an important lesson from China's unwillingness to share information during the early days of the SARS epidemic: "Processes of social and environmental change, including transnational migration, ecological destruction, and increasing international travel, had generated novel biological, social, and political risks—risks that transcended national borders and therefore . . . only a global system of rapidly shared epidemiological information could provide adequate warning to mitigate such risks."[56] But for such a system to work effectively, all national governments must be willing to actively participate.

It is ironic, therefore, that the first international conference on epidemic diseases (to which the WHO traces its origins) occurred in China, during the 1911 epidemic of pneumonic plague spreading from the China-Russia border (in the region then known as Manchuria). The meeting was sponsored by the Qing government's minister of public health and organized by Wu Lien-teh, an ethnically Chinese and British-trained doctor from Malaysia, who was also the first to promote not only quarantines, but also the use of face masks for medical workers and the general population as a public health measure to contain the outbreak of respiratory infectious diseases.[57] Wu's role and the state-making efforts he led in China would find significant echoes almost a century later in the aftermath of SARS.

During the first months of the SARS epidemic, however, the Chinese minister of health denied that SARS was a novel respiratory infectious disease, punted responsibility to the local and provincial levels, and suppressed the spread of negative information both domestically and abroad. This not only delayed international preparedness, but also laid the condition for hospitals to become new epicenters of SARS infection, as medical workers were not instructed on the need to quarantine SARS patients and their contacts and require rigorous use of masks and other personal protection equipment (PPE) when caring for SARS patients.[58]

As the epidemic continued to spread from Guangdong to other provinces, lower-level officials hesitated to report on the actual progress of the epidemic for fear of negative repercussions for their careers, and high-level officials prioritized maintaining economic growth and the appearance of stability at the cost of public well-being. There were a few exceptions, of course, and the most notable of them was Zhong Nanshan, a pulmonologist who directed the Guangzhou Institute of Respiratory Diseases. Zhong was at the front lines during the outbreak in Guangdong province, and as an expert in respiratory diseases, he insisted on treating the new disease as such, despite official protocols. He maintained contact with colleagues in Hong Kong and attempted to warn senior government officials, other doctors, and even the public that this outbreak was not controlled but appeared to be a respiratory infection that could become an epidemic.[59] But government officials remained unmoved and pressured him to stop spreading such information domestically and abroad. Their main concern was to maintain social and political stability, as information that hundreds of people were starting to die from "a strange contagious disease" was already triggering "panic" among the masses during February 2003, when the Chinese government notified the WHO that people started "emptying pharmaceutical stocks of any medicine they think may protect them."[60]

The turning point for the Chinese government to shift from censorship to international collaboration, and from denial to rigorous implementation of epidemic control measures, came when the WHO was finally allowed to visit China during late March 2003. At first, the WHO delegation was restricted from inspecting Guangdong province and even the hospitals in Beijing where SARS patients were actually being treated, so that the Chinese government could try to convince them that the outbreak was already contained. A retired medical doctor, however, exposed the cover-up by sending emails to news outlets in China, who did not report on the whistle-blower but leaked the information to *Time* magazine. Unable to maintain the cover-up any longer, the political tides shifted between different factions among the top leadership. The minister of health and the mayor of Beijing who favored the cover-up were replaced, and the government began collaborating with the WHO and rolling out drastic epidemic control measures.[61]

First, strict regulations were imposed on people's movement and social gatherings, and quarantines were implemented in various cities and regions where outbreaks were taking place. This strategy had already been successfully implemented in Zhejiang province, where the epidemiologist Li Lanjuan led efforts that addressed the epidemic as a respiratory infection.[62] Second, the protocol for medical treatment was officially revised, enforcing the use of face masks and other PPE in hospitals, and replacing antibiotics (prescribed for chlamydia and other bacterial infections) with treatments for respiratory infections caused by viruses. While this treatment regime was often implemented in conjunction with TCM, Zhong Nanshan was leading efforts to employ Western biomedical interventions like artificial ventilation and cortisone, and so he was brought to Beijing in April 2003 to report to the WHO on these effective measures to contain and treat the novel disease.[63] The effective integration of Western medicine with TCM in the treatment of many SARS cases "reinforced the Chinese government's patronage of TCM as an integral aspect of the nation's health care system."[64] But ultimately, as Zhong straddled the roles of a state-backed scientist, a doctor who could speak up from among the masses, and an expert who could dialogue with the international community, it was Zhong and his approach that gained most attention.[65] The Chinese government had to rebuild trust among the masses and the international community, and it did so through celebrations of Zhong, reinforcing popular faith in experts and biomedical sciences, and welding the need for modernization with the operational capacity of the state.

As the containment of SARS began to be celebrated, therefore, this victory was attributed to the work of scientists and the technology they wield. This propelled further expansion of domestic and international institutions of public health surveillance, including an "epidemic alarm system" placed under the auspices of a reinvigorated China CDC, modeled explicitly on the US CDC. Yet this system remained constrained by the hierarchical nature of Chinese governance, prohibiting municipal and provincial branches of the CDC or health commissions from declaring public health emergencies within their own jurisdictions, and preventing them from reporting outbreaks to the higher-level CDC and health commissions without approval of the municipal or provincial government.[66] In addition to institutional constraints, effective implementation of public health measures has often been undermined by the continued authority of older-generation directors of CDC agencies, who set priorities and conduct operations based upon their own career-advancement goals, political expediency, and need to maintain interpersonal relationships with government officials and business leaders.[67]

At the international level, moreover, the ability of the WHO to step in relatively quickly and successfully seemed to confirm "the effectiveness of international agencies with large bureaucracies and limited resources for action. But," as a team of British epidemiologists concluded, "it is difficult to escape the conclusion that the world community was very lucky this time round, given the very low transmissibility of the agent, plus the fact that fairly draconian public health measures could be put in place with great efficiency in Asian regions where the epidemic originated."[68] Rather than attributing the victory over SARS to modern statecraft, international collaborations, and the advancements of biomedical sciences, therefore, it would be more accurate to recognize the effectiveness of early twentieth century public health measures first implemented by Wu Lien-teh to contain the pneumonic plague in northeastern China in 1911 and the long history of TCM treatments and preventive measures.[69]

Nonetheless, the view that SARS was overcome by modern science and technology was mobilized to advance hospital construction, medical supply production (e.g., ventilators, masks, and other PPE), and pharmaceutical treatments for infectious diseases. Fever clinics were designed as separate additions to hospitals, which invested heavily in medical equipment of high technology and massive stocks of pharmaceuticals and medical supplies. In this way, the SARS outbreak accelerated a process that had been developing since market reforms began in China, with the privatization of hospitals and their operation for profit; promotion of high-tech equipment to enhance their reputation, competitiveness, and revenues from expensive exams; and incentivizing prescription of expensive drugs and medical devices for patients, yielding larger bonuses for healthcare professionals.[70] While this process of privatization of healthcare modernized urban hospitals, it simultaneously dismantled China's rural healthcare system, leading to a decentralized and highly fragmented system that contributes to the difficulty of coordination among various levels of government and medical practitioners in the event of an epidemic outbreak.[71] This fragmentation also expresses itself in the deepening of specialization among biomedical scientists and medical doctors, making it increasingly more difficult for them to grasp and address complex phenomena like the emergence of a novel disease, and even setting them in competition with each other for prestige and profits from the way problems and solutions are posed.

Ultimately, in shifting priorities from public health to profit-making, the transformation from the socialist goal of democratizing healthcare to the modernization of China's biomedical sciences and healthcare system through capitalist reforms also determines the priorities of public and private investment in treatments and vaccines. Remember, for example, that the high-risk efforts of "bat hunters" like Tian Junhua and virologists like Shi Zhengli were intended to be ultimately justified by the development of a vaccine. In the years after the SARS outbreak, several research teams "achieved promising results" in both animal studies and human trials, and the international scientific community reached a consensus that "the successful development of SARS vaccine appears feasible and worthwhile."[72] But as time passed, public attention drifted, and pharmaceutical companies and government agencies— within China and in other countries—shifted focus toward pharmaceutical treatments that could be more profitable, abandoning the effort to bring a SARS vaccine into production.[73] Even the 2012 MERS outbreak failed to reignite sufficient concern among state and corporate elites, leaving scientific teams without funds to test and manufacture a coronavirus vaccine.[74] Just like the neglect of strategies to prevent spillover of novel diseases from animals to humans, and transnational companies prioritizing pharmaceuticals that can be sold more profitably in the US and Europe over treatments for endemic diseases among the poor or vaccines for novel diseases,[75] the key factors that shape the "lessons learned" from the SARS epidemic are a feature of global capitalism itself. They are an entanglement of state and biomedical corporate interests that glorifies modern science and technology as the dominant way to address emergent diseases with pandemic potential. And they not only failed to prevent another novel coronavirus outbreak in 2019, but continue to overlook the structural conditions that drive the emergence of infectious diseases like COVID-19.

2   EMERGENCE

Wuhan, the capital of Hubei province, is the most populous and important city in central China. Sitting at the confluence of the Yangtze River and its largest tributary, Wuhan has served as a major transportation hub throughout Chinese history. The first railway bridge across the Yangtze was built there in 1957, consolidating its central position in China's transportation system. An early hub of the steel industry during the late Qing dynasty, and a major center of food processing and textile industry during the republican era, Wuhan was then selected as a core area for heavy industry development during the Maoist period. But since market- and export-oriented reforms began in the 1980s, industrial development in Wuhan and central China as a whole began to fall behind the coastal provinces.

It was only after the SARS epidemic, with the establishment of the "Rise of Central China Plan" of 2004, that state and capital interests coalesced again in a push to redevelop Wuhan, serving now as a fulcrum in China's efforts to connect its hinterlands with the global economy. Upon its important legacy of logistics, food processing, and heavy industry, a thick layer of the "new economy" was overlaid in Wuhan. It emphasized software, telecommunications, fine chemicals, biotechnology, and pharmaceuticals, alongside hundreds of related research institutes, including the Wuhan Institute of Virology (WIV). After years of preparation, Wuhan was also awarded status of "national civilized" and "hygienic city" in 2015, designations that increase real estate prices. This new round of urban expansion and industrial modernization in Wuhan explains why it could become the site for an infectious disease outbreak that could then become epidemic throughout China, and even a global pandemic, in such short time.

INTERMEDIARIES

We still don't know exactly how, where, and when a novel coronavirus spilled over to humans, triggering the current pandemic. But comparing the SARS-CoV-2 virus that causes COVID-19 to other known coronaviruses suggests this spillover may have occurred from bats through an intermediary species, as this passage could have facilitated genetic mutations that made the virus more easily contagious among humans.[1] This hypothesis emerged soon after the genetic sequence of the novel coronavirus was made public in early 2020, when epidemiological studies had already identified the Huanan Market as the main cluster of the earliest known cases of atypical pneumonia in Wuhan.[2] Just as wildlife or other animals traded in that market may have been an intermediary between bats and humans, Wuhan itself might have been an intermediary location in the global value chains of the exotic animal trade, linking some remote place (within China or beyond) to the dense networks of the global capitalist economy.

Various teams of virologists within China and from other countries raced to identify the likely reservoir and intermediary species, searching for the closest match between SARS-CoV-2 and coronaviruses known to be endemic among various animals. In the early stages of the epidemic, a team proposed pangolins carry the coronavirus with the closest match, another argued that the best match are ferrets or bamboo rats, yet another argued snakes or turtles, all of which appeared to have been sold—many of them illegally—in the Huanan Market.[3] "Soon scientists will know for sure which animal was the intermediary by sequencing the genetic code," a Chinese biologist at UC Irvine told me, "and then we just need to regulate trade of that particular wild animal more strictly." This blasé attitude is comforting to many, as it reassures trust in science, technology, and "good governance." But things are not so simple. In fact, this naïve trust reveals the arrogance that predominates among many scientists, who ignore the social complexity that is required to transform a "pathogen" into a *disease*, and thereby forecloses critique of the capitalist modernity that increases the spillover of new viruses from animals to humans.[4]

In order for a spillover from wild animals to trigger a pandemic, after all, remote hinterlands must be interconnected by increased human mobility and global logistics networks. Whatever animal was reservoir or intermediary to the first human infections with COVID-19, the disease needed to find its way into a large urban area that also served as transportation hub for national and international travel, so that a local outbreak could become a global pandemic.[5] China and Wuhan certainly fit this condition. In 2000, for example, China had 1.4 million kilometers of paved roads, and by 2019, this number more than tripled, reaching 4.8 million kilometers. Railway development progressed even faster, growing from 10,000 to 139,000 kilometers between 2000 and 2019, including 35,000 kilometers of high speed rail for passenger transport, all of it added since 2009. Due to these developments, travel times between Wuhan and Beijing or Guangzhou dropped from about twelve to four hours, and annual railway passengers increased from about 1 billion in 2000 to over 3.3 billion in 2018. The population of Wuhan increased from about 8 million in 2000 to over 11 million in 2019, and the number of high speed trains and flights connecting Wuhan to other parts of China and the world also increased dramatically. In 2000, Wuhan's main airport served 1.7 million passengers with 34,000 domestic flights. By 2018, over 27.1 million passengers traveled through Wuhan's airport on 203,000 flights, including sixty-three international routes. Regardless of how and where a new virus jumped species to infect humans, it is not simply bad luck or coincidence that a major transportation hub like Wuhan would host the first major outbreak of a pandemic.

This urban growth and industrial development are celebrated as evidence of China's modernization and the success of its policy to integrate central China into the globalized economy. But urbanization and industrialization are not inevitable. Rather they are an expression of a global eco-modernist development model that is highly dependent on international markets and capitalist profits, the sacrifice of farmland and local ecologies, and the degradation of the global environment through natural resource imports from remote regions and emission of pollution that causes chronic diseases and drives global climate change. The agglomeration of workers with poor healthcare also increases susceptibility to infectious diseases. The socio-ecological problems that render this development model unsustainable are well known,[6] but the way they also condition the emergence of pandemic diseases is not often factored into the calculation of this development model's costs and benefits.

Discounting these public health risks justifies the continued expansion of this modernist, urban-focused and industrial-dependent development model into the most remote corners of the earth. Here again, China leads global efforts through its poverty alleviation campaign domestically, and its Belt and Road Initiative for infra-structure construction abroad. These two efforts come together precisely in the expansion of infrastructure and agro-industrial development on China's remote borders, such as the provinces of Guangxi and Yunnan. Their mountainous terrain separating China from its neighbors in Southeast Asia have been one of the most remote fron-tiers in human history, where modern state-making efforts have faltered until recently.[7] Precisely for this reason, they have been recently targeted for development.[8]

China's poverty alleviation campaign, for example, included efforts to formalize and scale-up the farming of various sorts of wild animals, including bamboo rats.[9] Consumption of bamboo rats has increased in China, shifting from a minor cultural practice in southern China into a significant market. Given China's ongoing food safety crisis, and consumers' growing understanding that the rise in chronic illnesses like diabetes and heart disease are associated with modern dietary habits, demand for wild animal meat has increased among some individu-als.[10] This process is also driven by the rise in e-commerce and social media influencers, who promote such prac-tices widely for urban consumer markets and audi-ences.[11] Since bamboo rats eat mainly bamboo, and are increasingly domesticated in animal farms, their meat is considered to be more "pure" and free from toxins used in mainstream livestock industries.[12] Moreover, their fur and skin can be sold to the textile and fashion indus-tries.[13] As bamboo rats start to be raised year-round and in larger numbers, within some peasants' own homes or concentrated in larger-scale farms, and brought in greater numbers to wet markets in cities like Wuhan, it becomes increasingly possible for viruses to spill over to humans. Zhong Nanshan, famous for telling the truth about the SARS outbreak years before, indicated in an interview with China Central Television (CCTV) on January 20, 2020, that this was quite likely.[14] But given the usefulness of this process for poverty alleviation and other economic interests, and how some pangolin coronaviruses have a key protein that closely matches SARS-CoV-2, multiple Chinese actors have found it more convenient to focus on animals that are less often raised domestically with government support, but rather smuggled into China from abroad, such as pangolins.

Pangolin scales were historically used in East Asia for the production of traditional medicines, and their meat is also considered a delicacy.[15] Just as with bamboo rats, and as part of the broader expansion of consumerism and commodification of healthcare in China, the demand for pangolins has increased in recent years. Due to accelerated hunting, wild pangolins virtually disappeared from China by the 2000s, becoming commercially extinct there and declared a critically endangered species in surrounding countries.[16] Consequently, the growing Chinese demand for pangolins began to be supplied by imports from Southeast Asia and Africa, transforming them into the most trafficked mammal in the world.[17] The inauguration of new roads and railroads connecting

China to Southeast Asia as part of the Belt and Road Initiative, and the increased extraction and export of various commodities from Africa to China, are the material foundation upon which the smuggling of pangolins and their scales can be clandestinely inserted. And as with attribution of SARS to civets in 2003, the hypothesis that pangolins or other wild animals may have played a role in the current pandemic led to a crackdown on markets selling wild animals, culling of certain species raised in captivity for commercial use, and stricter enforcement of antitrafficking regulations. But such practices often drive wildlife smuggling further underground, and there is little evidence these efforts will lead to actual pandemic prevention in the long term.[18]

By early 2021, the leading hypothesis of the joint WHO-China team investigating the origins of COVID-19 (considered to be "likely to very likely") involves farmed wild animals as an intermediary for the spillover to humans, but much more investigation is still required to confirm it.[19] One might wonder, if farmed bamboo rats or smuggled pangolins were the intermediary species in the spillover of the coronavirus that causes COVID-19, why didn't the earliest outbreaks of the disease occur around Guangzhou (like SARS), where wild animal consumption is more prominent than in Wuhan, and which still serves as a main port-of-entry for wildlife smuggled through international shipments? Or why didn't the earliest outbreaks occur in other major cities in southern China like Kunming, Nanning, or Changsha, which sit between Wuhan and the mountainous borders with Southeast Asia through which smuggling routes pass and where most wild animal production for poverty alleviation campaigns take place? These questions assume novel diseases emerge from a single spillover event in a particular place. But this is not necessarily the case, as it might take multiple mutations and instances of cross-species spillover for a virus to adapt well enough to humans so that it can begin to spread among us.[20] So the direct ancestor of SARS-CoV-2 may have been circulating in southern China for some time before it finally mutated into the form that caused the outbreak in Wuhan and became epidemic from there.

EXPOSURES

The second hypothesis the joint WHO-China team identifies for further investigation (considered to be "possible to likely") involves a direct spillover from a host animal species (such as bats) to humans.[21] Without an intermediary animal through which additional mutations could occur, this process requires longer-term exposure of humans to the hosts carrying the novel coronavirus, resulting in their recombination into a strain that is infectious among humans ourselves. These conditions might be more difficult to find than the transnational networks of pangolin smuggling and the thousands of new wild animal farms in China's poor periphery, but they exist in the caves and mines of southwestern China and elsewhere. In fact, the bat coronavirus most similar to SARS-CoV-2 was found precisely in a place like this by Shi Zhengli's team in 2012 in Yunnan, and the second-closest was found in 2020 by another team ninety-five miles away in Yunnan as well, and other very similar SARS-like viruses have also been found among bats in Thailand and Cambodia.[22]

This story begins with gold and nickel. Their prices were rising steadily during the 2000s and reached record heights after the 2008–2009 global financial crisis. Given record high prices from 2010 to 2015, and the relative lack of economic opportunity for poor peasants in rural areas, various caves and abandoned mines were being reoccupied throughout China and Southeast Asia for mineral exploration. Mojiang county in Yunnan province, with a long history of mining, was one of these places.[23] Output from gold mining in Mojiang increased from 858 kilograms in 2006 to 1,090 kilograms in 2012, and peaked at 1,535 kilograms in 2014. Nickel mining restarted in 2006 and also peaked at about 1,500 tons in 2014 as well.[24] In April 2012, in the midst of this mining boom, six men were hired to clean bat droppings from a cave in Tongguan town, Mojiang county, either to use the bat guano as fertilizer or to enable its conversion into a profitable mine.

The miners encountered a large number of bats and were significantly exposed to their droppings. All six men fell severely ill within two weeks of working in the mine, presenting high fever, dry cough, difficulty breathing, muscle pain, and other symptoms of atypical pneumonia, including evidence from CT scans of ground glass opacities in their lungs[25]—symptoms that match what we now know to be COVID-19. After some of them were treated with antibiotics in local clinics but showed no improvement, they were admitted to hospitals in nearby Yuxi city. Between April 25 and 27, 2012, the five most severe cases were transferred to the intensive care unit (ICU) of the First Affiliated Hospital of the Kunming Medical University, the best hospital in the province. The sixth patient who was not so severe was transferred to the respiratory unit of the same hospital on May 2. They were tested for influenza, tuberculosis, other likely diseases, and two of them were even tested for SARS. But laboratory results were all negative, except for two patients who had hepatitis, and one who had the Epstein-Barr virus as well. All patients were initially treated with corticosteroids, antibiotics, and antifungal medications, except for the last one who did not receive antifungal medications. Three of the most severe cases were also placed on artificial ventilation. The oldest man was sixty-three years old and had hepatitis and tumors, and despite treatment he passed away within twelve days of admittance to the ICU. The second who passed away was forty-two, also had hepatitis, and died after forty-eight days of treatment. The third who passed away was forty-five, had no underlying health conditions, and died much later, after 109 days of treatment. Unlike the others who died before him, however, this patient also started to receive treatment with antivirals, as it was clear that antibiotics and antifungal medications were not having any positive effect.

This change in treatment was made upon remote consultation with Zhong Nanshan from Guangzhou. The oldest patient who survived was forty-six years old, after 107 days in the hospital, which included antiviral treatment as well. The two others who survived were younger (thirty and thirty-two years old) and had worked only four days in the bat-infested mine, replacing the older men who had already spent fourteen days working there when they first became ill. Their general condition was much better than the others, and one of them was treated with antibiotics and antifungal medicines, while the other was treated with antibiotics and antiviral medicines directly.

The case of the Mojiang miners resembles SARS and COVID-19. In his remote consultation, Zhong Nanshan explicitly stated that he suspected viral (not fungal) infections and suggested not only shifting treatment to antivirals, but also collecting biological samples for testing for SARS infection and antibodies, and coordinating with the Kunming Zoology Institute to identify the specific bats encountered by the miners. The doctors in Kunming were only able to collect biological samples from four of the patients and sent these samples to Zhong and the WIV for testing. All four samples tested positive for coronavirus antibodies. The Kunming Zoology Institute soon identified the bats in the Mojiang mine as horseshoe bats (*Rhinolophus*), known to carry many varieties of SARS-like coronaviruses.[26] Thus, Dr. Li Xu, who treated the Mojiang miners and who wrote the only known clinical research about their case, concluded that the patients suffered from an infection by "a SARS-like coronavirus or bat-like SARS coronavirus" acquired through exposure to horseshoe bats in the Mojiang mine.[27]

Li Xu's suspicion that the Mojiang miners succumbed to an unknown SARS-like coronavirus led several research teams to go investigate the mine and its bats. After the Kunming Zoology Institute, a second team from the Peking Union Medical College, the Institute of Pathogen Biology in Beijing, and the Yunnan Institute of Parasitic Diseases surveyed the mine and identified a new strain of henipavirus in rats, but could not establish a connection with the infected miners.[28] Huang Canping, who was conducting his PhD research at the China CDC, went to Mojiang to investigate the mine in 2014. With support from the Yunnan and Mojiang CDCs, they captured one rat and eighty-seven bats and identified bat coronaviruses HKU7 and HKU8 in their samples. However, Huang and this third team were not able to draw any connection between those viruses and the case of the miners, which he concluded to remain "mysterious."[29] Ultimately, Huang noted that other people had gone into the same mine but did not appear to get sick, so "it is necessary to conduct long-term monitoring of [the mine] in order to understand the mutations and evolution of specific environment and animal groups, as well as the possibility of cross-species infection."[30]

The fourth team that surveyed the mine was led by Shi Zhengli from the WIV. At that time, they were researching bat-infested caves in Jinning county, about 100 miles northeast of the mine in Mojiang where the miners were infected and where they also discovered SARS-like coronaviruses in 2012.[31] Shi's team went to Mojiang while some of the miners were still hospitalized and sampled 276 bats from what they called "an abandoned mineshaft."[32] They identified various coronaviruses, including previously unknown strains, one of which was described as "SARS-like," and it remains the closest known match to the coronavirus that causes COVID-19, with a 96.2% similarity.[33] Also, importantly, they identified a large diversity of bat species living in high densities in that cave and a high frequency of bats infected with more than one variety of coronavirus, "which may result in recombination and acceleration of coronavirus evolution."[34] In other words, they found conditions that could facilitate the direct transmission of a novel coronavirus from bats to humans and could accelerate its mutation into a strain that could spread more easily among humans.

But despite the clinical features of the Mojiang miners, and the strong suspicion their condition resulted from a SARS-like coronavirus infection, it appears no report was issued of atypical pneumonia, or another SARS-like disease, despite the policy and institutional structures set up in 2007 after the SARS outbreak for precisely such situations (instructing all medical institutions to report any case of atypical pneumonia to the local CDC and health commission within twenty-four hours of diagnosis, which should in turn report to higher levels within twenty-four hours of receiving that notice). After reviewing public documents from the Yunnan Province Health Commission, Yunnan Provincial CDC, and Mojiang county government on all infectious disease outbreaks (including reports of unknown disease outbreaks) from 2012, I found no record of the Mojiang miners incident. In November 2012, however, the Yunnan Province Health Commission issued a "notice on further strengthening the diagnosis, reporting, and disposal of cases of pneumonia of unknown origin," reinforcing the 2007 national regulations.[35] Moreover, issues related to transparency and industrial accidents began to feature prominently in Mojiang county public government records starting in late 2012, leading to a crackdown in 2016 on illegal mining and other activities considered to present high risk for public health.[36] It is unclear whether internal investigations by government agencies were taking place alongside the scientific research on caves in the region, but in retrospect this incident might contribute crucial information for the investigation of a key hypothesis posed by the joint WHO-China team on the possible evolution of SARS-CoV-2.

Shi Zhengli and her team from the WIV could also elucidate more about their research in Mojiang. Their research concludes that, since "the two highly pathogenic human coronaviruses (SARS-CoV and MERS-CoV) in this genus originated from bats, attention should be particularly paid to these lineages of bat coronaviruses."[37] Yet nowhere in their scientific publications do they mention that six men who were exposed to the bats in that same mine became ill (and three even died) with a SARS-like disease. Instead, Shi stated that the Mojiang miners did not suffer from a viral disease at all, or even an atypical pneumonia of unknown origin, but rather from simple fungal infections. In an interview with the *Scientific American* from June 2020, Shi emphasized that "the mine shaft stunk like hell [because] bat guano, *covered in fungus*, littered the cave."[38] The *Scientific American* continues with the claim that "although the fungus turned out to be the pathogen that had sickened the miners, she says it would have been only a matter of time before they caught the coronaviruses if the mine had not been promptly shut."[39] It is not clear what evidence Shi Zhengli or the *Scientific American* used for the claim that it was a fungal, and not viral infection, that affected the Mojiang miners.

This makes for a rather awkward narrative, which has encouraged some scholars to ask why Shi and her team haven't been more transparent about the circumstances in which they identified COVID-19's closest known relative, and which has even pushed other scholars to suggest that COVID-19 may have emerged in Wuhan due to a laboratory incident at the WIV itself, or through a bungled collaboration with the Wuhan CDC,[40] whose "laboratory moved on 2nd December 2019 to a new location near the Huanan market [and] such moves can be disruptive for the operations of any laboratory," according to the joint WHO-China report on the origins of COVID-19.[41] Moreover, just like Tian Junhua in chapter 1 was accidentally exposed to bat urine during one of his virus-hunting expeditions, it is also possible that the scientists may have become accidentally exposed during an expedition to the bat caves in Yunnan or elsewhere and inadvertently brought the infection back to Wuhan without even carrying symptoms. The second closest known relative to SARS-CoV-2 was recently identified among bats in the Xishuangbanna Tropical Botanical Garden in Yunnan province, where researcher-turned-science-educator Zhang Jinshuo accompanied tourist groups into bat caves for a popular TV entertainment show in 2014, handling fresh bat feces without even wearing gloves.[42] His team is also shown handling live bats without gloves in scientific publications of their own from 2008.[43]

The possibility that COVID-19 emerged through research-related incidents (especially a "lab leak") has become a highly politicized topic, embroiled with geopolitical tensions that will be discussed in subsequent chapters. And as such, this possibility is often addressed and dismissed as a mere "conspiracy theory" alongside discredited scenarios, such as the artificial manipulation of the precursor to the COVID-19 coronavirus to deliberately increase its virulence and its release as an intentional act of biological warfare.[44] Yet the possibility of research-related incidents is not a "conspiracy," but rather a legitimate hypothesis that the joint WHO-China team considered in its investigation of the origins of COVID-19. While the team concluded that "introduction through a laboratory incident [is] extremely unlikely,"[45] other research-related exposures (e.g., accidental infection during a virus-hunting expedition) remain part of the investigation of possible pathways of direct zoonotic spillover worldwide. But a confirmation of this hypothesis would undermine the legitimacy of the most prominent approaches to research on emerging infectious diseases, which are dependent upon invasive surveillance of wildlife worldwide and which combine political and private sector interests all around the world (e.g., EcoHealth Alliance and the Global Virome Project). Given this dilemma, therefore, it is unsurprising that there hasn't been much research in this direction so far, even though the joint WHO-China report calls to "further investigate possible direct zoonotic introduction" pathways.[46] Moreover, this dilemma is embodied in the joint WHO-China study recommendation that emphasizes the need for more "genomic surveys and structured serosurveys of high-risk potential reservoir hosts and their human contacts,"[47] which increases the human-wildlife interface and goes against scientific warnings that "roosting sites should be protected, *even from researchers*, so that bats are not disturbed."[48]

Still, there is an international scientific consensus that the coronavirus strain that causes COVID-19 is most closely related to the coronavirus that Shi's team discovered in the same Mojiang mine where the miners were infected in 2012 and that other SARS-like coronaviruses are also endemic to bats living in the same region of Yunnan province.[49] Whether or not COVID-19 emerged due to a research-related accident, however, the structural conditions that give rise to emergent diseases like this remain the same. And so, it is possible to theorize an even more likely trajectory for novel coronaviruses to travel from remote mountains to the metropolis of Wuhan without reference to any research-related incidents as well.[50]

After their discovery of SARS-like coronavirus strains in Yunnan, Shi's team set out to examine whether local populations might display signs of exposure to coronavirus diseases. In 2015, they tested 218 people from villages located between 1 and 6 kilometers from the caves where they found SARS-like coronaviruses among bats in Jinning county and found that six people (2.7% of their sample) tested positive for SARS antibodies, and that all these individuals were among the 9% in their total sample that reported bats flying close to their homes.[51] None of these individuals reported symptoms of SARS in the previous year, leading Shi and her team to conclude their infections occurred much earlier or that they experienced mild or no symptoms of the infection. They interpreted these results as showing that "spillover is a rare event," yet still maintained the possibility that more individuals living in proximity to bat colonies may have also been exposed in the past, but their antibodies waned with time.[52]

Therefore, it seems likely that people living in Yunnan's mountains and the surrounding region may have been exposed to SARS-like coronaviruses for quite some time.[53] Given how difficult transportation across those mountainous regions has been throughout history, local spillovers in the past would not necessarily trigger regional epidemics, much less global pandemics.[54] This began to change when the G8511 highway connecting Mojiang county to the provincial capital of Kunming was completed in 2003, followed by dramatic expansion of rail networks connecting Kunming and other cities in Yunnan to the Laos and Vietnam borders since the 2000s. Since then, the Hani and other ethnic minority people inhabiting Mojiang and neighboring counties extended their migrations from their own region to the factories of Guangdong and other major cities elsewhere in southern and central China,[55] and cross-border migrations across Southeast Asia and China increased infectious disease prevalence in the region.[56] Expansion of road and rail networks also increased the fragmentation of natural habitats for bats and other wild animals in the region, concentrating wildlife into increasingly smaller areas and expanding the human-wildlife interface.[57] Moreover, as logistics infrastructure improved, mining and e-commerce have increased dramatically during the past decade.[58] And the same roads, railroads, and flights that facilitate commodity flows have also enabled a growing influx of tourists seeking to enjoy the remnants of southern China's and Southeast Asia's wilderness—particularly the Xishuangbanna Tropical Botanical Garden where the second-closest known relative of SARS-CoV-2 was identified and countries like Thailand and Cambodia where other closely related coronaviruses have also been found—and such rural tourism is increasingly promoted as yet another form of poverty alleviation for remote mountainous areas across the region.[59] In Mojiang, for example, the number of tourists visiting annually increased from 1.27 million in

2006 to 2.14 million in 2015, and revenues from tourism increased from 192 million RMB to 340 million RMB during the same period.[60] Last but not least, there is evidence that both mining activities and rural tourism are clustering in biodiversity hot spots in recent years.[61] Combined, these factors make it increasingly more likely that the spillover of a novel coronavirus from bats to people in Yunnan province or the surrounding region could transmit a new disease from remote villages to major urban centers.

⌐Whether directly from bats to humans, or indirectly through an intermediary species increasingly farmed in the region like bamboo rats, this gradual and complex path for novel coronaviruses to emerge from the mountains of Yunnan or the surrounding region and trigger the first major outbreak in Wuhan is my leading hypothesis.[62] And in fact, a genetic study of the earliest samples of SARS-CoV-2 suggests that strains circulating not only in Wuhan, but also in Guangdong during early 2020 were more genetically similar to the strains found in Yunnan's bats than those found among the majority of Wuhan's COVID-19 patients at the time.[63] Thus, it is possible to theorize that SARS-like coronaviruses from Yunnan or elsewhere in the region, descendant from or similar to the one that infected the Mojiang miners in 2012 and that Shi's team found among the residents of Jinning county in 2015, were circulating throughout southern China for a few years and underwent a genetic mutation in Wuhan sometime in November or December 2019 that increased their capacity to spread among humans. This might have occurred with the virus jumping species back-and-forth between humans, wildlife, and other animals farmed throughout the region and sold at wet markets or even supermarkets. After all, such large-scale indoor market environments and their transportation networks, where multiple animals are concentrated and kept in conditions that increase their susceptibility to infection, may also accelerate the mutation and recombination of viruses.[64] This could have transformed a relatively mild or slow-paced infectious disease circulating throughout southern China into the highly contagious and severe disease we now call COVID-19, which became epidemic with a super-spreader event in downtown Wuhan.

OUTBREAKS

Whatever specific way the novel coronavirus emerged, it was only in December 2019 that enough cases of atypical pneumonia began to be detected in Wuhan for doctors to identify an outbreak of an unknown disease. Retroactive investigation by the joint WHO-China study on the origins of COVID-19 indicates the onset of the epidemic is estimated to have taken place "sometime between mid-November and early December."[65]

The earliest epidemiological studies identified four in   luals who started to experience symptoms of pneu-
       etween December 1 and 10 and were hospitalized
          ber 16 in Wuhan.[66] They underwent clinical

and laboratory examination and treatment for pneumonia, and since no cause was identified for their condition and their symptoms showed no improvement after three to five days of treatment, the hospitals treating them should have reported the cases to the Wuhan CDC as a "pneumonia of unknown etiology" (i.e., unknown origin) sometime between December 19 and 21.[67] Yet this was a period of much uncertainty and confusion, so it is not clear whether these cases were not reported right away according to the protocols established after the SARS epidemic, or if they were reported to the district and/or municipal CDC in Wuhan, but the municipal or provincial health commissions or governments did not pass on the report to the national CDC.[68]

Between December 22 and 26, as more patients continued to arrive with similar symptoms in several hospitals in Wuhan, samples from the first few patients were already being sent to various laboratories, public and private, across China for examination.[69] Most Chinese media sources indicate that the first report from a hospital to the Wuhan city and Hubei province CDC was made on or soon after December 27, initiated by Dr. Zhang Jixian,[70] but the national CDC only confirms this report was received at the municipal and/or provincial levels by December 29.[71] By then, hospitals in Wuhan were starting to receive results from the samples sent to laboratories in Guangzhou, Shenzhen, and Beijing, which reported between December 27 and 30 that it appeared those samples contained a new strain of a SARS-like coronavirus, or perhaps even SARS itself, and new samples were then taken from patients and sent to the WIV for further examination.[72]

Also on December 30, the Wuhan Municipal Health Commission issued its first two official instructions to the city's healthcare system, alerting them to look for cases of infectious pneumonia, send clinical and epidemiological data of such cases from the past week to the Wuhan Health Commission, maintain rigorous protocols, training, and discipline to prevent the spread of infection within the hospital, and prohibiting medical staff and institutes from making public statements without permission.[73] However, that day a few doctors had already started to circulate these notices and the results from the laboratory exams through social media, indicating there might be an outbreak of SARS or a SARS-like disease in Wuhan.[74]

Finally, on December 31, as this first alarm circulated in social media, the Wuhan Municipal Health Commission made a public statement about the matter. It alerted the public that twenty-seven cases of pneumonia were identified in connection with the Huanan Market and advised the city's residents to wear masks in public, avoid crowded places with poor air circulation, and seek medical care when feeling symptoms of pneumonia.[75] In an attempt to avoid causing panic, the press release did not draw a connection with SARS and emphasized that there were no signs of human-to-human transmission, no healthcare workers were infected, and that the outbreak was controllable.[76]

That same day, the Wuhan government collected biological samples from the Huanan Market and disinfected certain areas without notice to the public or market operators, the National Health Commission sent a team for inspection to Wuhan, and the first national media reports emerged about the outbreak of pneumonia of unknown origin in Wuhan.[77] Last but not least, the Chinese government informed the WHO and neighboring countries.[78] It was clear the outbreak had become an emergency.

3 EMERGENCY

The period between New Year and the lockdown of Wuhan on Spring Festival Eve (January 23) was crucial and remains subject to much debate. Mainstream Chinese narratives emphasize the speed, transparency, and effectiveness of government action. "On the 4th day after the epidemic was reported," states the editor of the influential *Beijing Daily*, "the nation was mobilized for a people's war and race against the virus."[1] Those sympathetic to the Chinese government share these views. "Officials from Beijing arrived in Wuhan within five days of the first sign of a problem," Vijay Prashad indicates and argues further that "there is no evidence the Chinese government systematically suppressed information."[2] Yet there are competing narratives that question this positive assessment and critique certain actions and inactions of the Chinese state and society that undermined effective public health responses early on, when the COVID-19 outbreak might have been contained within Wuhan and neighboring areas of Hubei province.

To be clear, these critiques are distinct from the crude anti-China rhetoric spewed by Donald Trump and others like him in the US and other countries, and involve objective assessments from investigative journalists and social science scholars from within China and beyond. A group of Chinese scholars based in Nanjing, Shanghai, and Australia, for example, argue that government censorship and disinformation during this period, combined with a lack of local autonomy for public health management and the privatization of the healthcare system, caused doctors and the masses to be unprepared in Wuhan and delayed for thirty-four days an appropriate response to the crisis.[3] In addition, some high-level officials from China's healthcare apparatus indicate lower-level officials withheld crucial information from decision-makers and refused to implement recommendations early enough, and later in February party leaders in Wuhan and Hubei province were sacked for mismanaging the emergency, admitting they should have acted sooner and more effectively.[4]

Therefore, it is important to examine carefully and objectively the events that unfolded during this crucial period, considering the actions taken (and not taken) by various branches of the state apparatus at the local, provincial, and national levels, alongside the role of numerous other actors in Chinese society, including doctors, scientists, business leaders, and the nameless masses.

Moreover, it is also necessary to evaluate these actions in light of important developments taking place at the same time elsewhere in the world, particularly when such developments may have directly affected the course of the epidemic in China. After all, an emergency might mean different things to different people. Thus, the discussion about whether the Chinese government responded to the crisis within four or thirty-four days is not a simple empirical question, but rather depends on when we start to count the "first sign of a problem" and what is considered to be an appropriate emergency response, given the dilemma of balancing a quick response without causing unnecessary panic.

COVER-UPS

On New Year's Eve 2019, a hospital director and the supervision department at the Wuhan Central Hospital reprimanded Li Wenliang, an ophthalmologist, for circulating WeChat messages to a group of 150 doctors warning that laboratory tests from patients with atypical pneumonia at his hospital indicated the disease might be SARS. The next day, January 1, they also reprimanded Ai Fen, director of the emergency department, who reported cases of "pneumonia of unknown origin" the previous day, but also took the original picture of the laboratory report, circled the word *SARS*, and shared it with a colleague at another hospital. By that evening, the picture was circulating among various doctors in Wuhan, including through Li Wenliang's messages. In line with the Wuhan Health Commission's ordinance from December 30, the hospital administration instructed both Li and Ai that no information could be shared, except through direct conversation with other staff caring for those specific patients. Meanwhile, the Wuhan police department launched an investigation of eight individuals for "spreading false rumors."[5]

Still on January 1, 2020, the Wuhan CDC temporarily closed down the Huanan Market for disinfection and collection of biological samples, without making any public statement about the matter, and the National Health Commission (NHC) established a leading group that would meet daily to coordinate the response to the epidemic. Meanwhile, the Hubei Health Commission contacted the private laboratories that had received samples of the novel coronavirus (and begun to identify it as SARS-like) to instruct them to destroy the samples they received, withhold all data and information about them, and if any further samples were received from Wuhan, they should not test them but report directly to the Hubei Health Commission.[6]

On January 3, the NHC provided its first report to the WHO and issued their first plan for "diagnosis and treatment of viral pneumonia of unexplained cause" jointly with the Hubei Health Commission. Simultaneously, however, the NHC also restricted regulations on research about the novel coronavirus, limiting it exclusively to central government-controlled laboratories. This cut off the work of provincial-level government laboratories, private laboratories, university laboratories, and even research institutes like the Wuhan Institute of Virology (WIV) that were already identifying the genetic sequence of the novel coronavirus, preventing them from publishing any results as they became available during the first few days of January.[7] Still on January 3, Li Wenliang was summoned to the police bureau to sign a confession of "spreading false rumors" and promise he would stop doing so, and only then were epidemiological investigations of the Huanan Market launched, that is, two days after it had already been closed for disinfection.[8]

On January 5, the full genetic sequence of the novel coronavirus was reported to the NHC by Zhang Yong-zhen's team in Shanghai, alerting the NHC that since it was SARS-like, "relevant prevention and control measures" needed to be implemented immediately.[9] But despite this warning, the China CDC reported that day that there were "no clear signs of human-to-human transmission" and that no healthcare workers were infected.[10] The previous day, George Fu Gao, the head of the China CDC, spoke personally with the director of the US CDC on the phone to discuss the epidemic and possible ways to cooperate in its control. Evidently, while the Chinese government was not fully censoring information about the outbreak from the WHO and other international audiences, as it had done during the SARS outbreak before, various government agencies from the central government down to the provincial and municipal levels were repressing information from doctors and scientists domestically. It seems this was an attempt to regulate the content and flow of information, particularly for domestic audiences, who only received small bits of information about the emergency unfolding in Wuhan. This information was easily lost amidst the usual torrent of nationalist and consumerist advertisement that dominates China's mainstream media, particularly in the lead up to the Spring Festival.[11]

It is important to underscore the cultural and political significance of this time of year. The Spring Festival, held on the Lunar New Year, is the most important and longest holiday in China, when students, migrant workers, and other professionals are able to travel back to their hometown for extended family gatherings, and also when Chinese families travel for tourism everywhere. Since the market reforms and rise of consumerism in recent decades, the weeks leading up to Spring Festival also have become an important shopping season, characterized by major banquets among communities and extended family. In other words, this is the peak season for small vendors and food markets like Huanan.

Moreover, as a period of transition in the lunar calendar year, it is also a time when the Chinese government and Communist Party hold their most important meetings for evaluating work during the previous year, and set policy goals, promotions, and priorities for the following year. These annual "two meetings" are staggered, starting with municipal government and party meetings, followed by provincial-level meetings prior to the Spring Festival, and finally convening national-level meetings in Beijing soon afterward. So the entire period surrounding the Spring Festival is also one of the most politically sensitive times in China, when the top priority for all government officials is to maintain stability, avoid public discontent, and prevent any trouble that could jeopardize their promotions and policy proposals. It is an especially unfortunate time for the outbreak of an unknown disease, therefore, as people are traveling more than at any other time in the year, and the authorities do not want to create any unnecessary public alarm that might destabilize the political and commercial activities culminating at that moment.[12]

But as more and more people fell ill and "rumors" continued to spread through social media and word-of-mouth, including information from healthcare workers themselves, it became increasingly difficult for the various levels of government to conceal the fact that something was wrong in Wuhan. The government-controlled media presented almost no information about the growing emergency, even as the national CDC activated its second-highest emergency procedures on January 6. High-level officials knew lower-level officials might withhold negative information from them, particularly as Wuhan held its two meetings of the party and government from January 6 to 10, followed by the two provincial-level meetings in Hubei from January 11 to 17. Thus, the central government's department of discipline and inspection launched an investigation on the whistle-blower incidents on January 7, and on January 8 the NHC sent a second delegation to Wuhan. Unlike the first delegation sent on December 30, which only met with local officials to learn from them about the situation, this second delegation planned to stay a few days and inspect hospitals directly.

The key question was how contagious this disease might be, as a slow-spreading disease might be contained in Wuhan without much public alarm, but a highly contagious outbreak was certain to trigger a national epidemic (and even global pandemic) if forceful public health measures were not implemented quickly enough. As most early cases clustered around the Huanan Market, the hypothesis that the disease was only acquired through direct contact with an infected animal encouraged the more optimistic assessment, while any evidence of human-to-human transmission, such as healthcare workers becoming infected, would force the conclusion that vigorous and very public measures were immediately required.

By the time the second NHC delegation arrived in Wuhan, in the midst of the two meetings at the city level, healthcare workers were already infected, including a doctor who was being treated at a hospital inspected by the delegation. However, as members of that delegation reported afterward, they were not informed by the directors of the hospital that a doctor there was already hospitalized with atypical pneumonia.[13] Still, there were several patients with no known connection to the Huanan

Market among the earliest confirmed cases, and the delegation also noted that delays in diagnostic testing due to limited laboratory supplies made it harder to identify cases that might provide evidence of human-to-human transmission.[14] Nonetheless, the NHC's own January 3 directive maintained that only cases with symptoms of pneumonia, laboratory confirmation of infection by coronavirus, *and also* exposure to the Huanan Market or another confirmed patient could be officially declared a "confirmed" case of the novel coronavirus disease, effectively locking most patients that would demonstrate human-to-human transmission into the category of "suspected" but unconfirmed cases.

Moreover, on January 10 a team of scientists from Guangdong province and Hong Kong identified a cluster of cases in a family that had traveled from Wuhan to Shenzhen, Guangdong province, and which included an infected family member who had not traveled to Wuhan, proving human-to-human transmission.[15] By January 11, there were at least seven healthcare workers infected in Wuhan, accounting for about 3% of all confirmed cases at the time, as high-level officials from the China and Hubei CDC themselves would admit in a scientific research article published merely eighteen days later in the highly influential *New England Journal of Medicine.*[16] In the same article, they even reported that human-to-human transmission had already occurred among cases from December.

Yet on January 10, the China CDC was still publicly reporting that no healthcare workers were infected, and on January 11 that "no clear evidence" of human-to-human transmission was found during the inspection of Wuhan.[17] Despite the mounting evidence, therefore, the official conclusion was that the outbreak was "manageable and controllable" without more drastic interventions. When the second NHC delegation completed their mission, the two meetings at the Hubei provincial level were beginning, and delegation members were unable to meet in person with Hubei's top leadership to emphasize their recommendations for more rigorous epidemic control measures, which included implementation of temperature checks at Wuhan's airport and train stations, and recommendations that people avoid crowds and social gatherings.[18]

However, once the second NHC delegation departed and the provincial-level government and party meetings commenced, the Hubei Health Commission halted disclosure of any new cases of infection by the novel coronavirus for the entire week of their meetings and decided not to enforce the recommendations of the NHC. The national CDC upgraded its emergency response procedures to the highest level on January 15, underscoring the recommendations made by the NHC delegation.[19] Yet there were no public announcements from the Wuhan and Hubei governments instructing people to avoid crowds and no efforts to halt large-scale social gatherings. On January 18, for example, a pre–Spring Festival banquet was allowed to take place at a residential community that gathered about 40,000 individuals, many of them elderly people who were already known to be the most vulnerable to pneumonia. Tragically, the banquet was later identified as a super-spreader event for the COVID-19 epidemic in Wuhan.[20] Rather than simply the result of cover-ups, however, this event demonstrates how state and capitalist interests become entangled in "maintaining stability," as real estate developers and local officials organize such community events jointly, leveraging the celebrations to improve their reputations, profits, and careers, while the masses revel in consumerism. Thus, it wasn't because information about the outbreak was censored that the gathering took place, as there were multiple interests in going ahead with the event at a point when the situation was still unclear.

This entanglement of political and economic interests also coalesced around two major events in Wuhan during those days. The first was another inspection by the NHC on January 16, focused on food safety and public hygiene at markets like Huanan, upon which Wuhan's continued official status as a "national civilized and hygienic city" depended, favoring its real estate market and status among China's most important cities. The second event was the Hubei Spring Reunion Gala on January 21, when top government officials from the province gather with prominent movie stars, TV personalities, and other artists who entertain the masses through live performances and rake in huge profits from TV advertisements and other commercials. Given the importance of both events for local elites, none of them had much interest to raise alarms that might force their cancellation.

Everyone certainly hoped this outbreak was just a small incident that could be contained, like some "false alarms" that had occurred in previous years, without triggering panic. And similar entanglement of interests might have also taken place at higher levels of governance. One of the most important issues under consideration by the State Council in early January, for example, was the "phase one" agreement with the US government to roll back the trade war, which was only cinched on January 15. As long as the epidemic remained a "local issue," therefore, central government officials could continue to pursue this top-priority deal without hindrances. In this context, while the situation remained unclear, state and business leaders had a combined interest in deemphasizing information about the outbreak and stalling on public health measures that might indicate a problem was at hand and disrupt these political and economic activities.

These state and capitalist interests also became entangled in the way hospital directors and political leaders responded to the growing emergency. As most hospitals were privatized, and even public institutions were pressured to demonstrate profitable operations, hospital administrations had no interest in receiving patients with a known connection to the Huanan Market, as cost-benefit calculations encouraged them to redirect "suspicious" patients to other hospitals.[21] Moreover, in order to cut costs, most hospitals had not stocked up sufficient PPE for an emergency like this, and hospital directors began to instruct their staff *not* to use full sets of PPE to avoid causing panic among its patients/customers. After all, rumors continued to circulate in social media and through word-of-mouth that a "mysterious disease" was spreading throughout the city and beyond, and would-be customers might avoid hospitals that seemed to be hosting infected patients. Consequently, doctors like Ai Fen and Zhang Jixian (who were concerned about the risks they were facing) had to procure additional masks, goggles, and full-body gowns for themselves and their staff at their own expense, and instruct their staff to wear the gowns *inside* their lab coats to avoid reprimand from the hospital administration.[22]

Another key recommendation from the second NHC delegation that was ignored by the Wuhan and Hubei governments was temperature checks at airports and train stations. Such measures had already been initiated in Singapore and Hong Kong for all travelers from Wuhan since January 3 and 4 respectively, but were not in fact taking place at Wuhan's airport and train station on January 14.[23] When cases of COVID-19 started to be confirmed outside China, the first in Thailand on January 13 and the second in Japan on January 15, this became a major challenge for the Chinese government at all levels.[24] Combined with pressure from certain experts within the China CDC and NHC and popular discontent, the China CDC admitted on January 14 that "limited human-to-human transmission is not excluded" but still maintained that even though "the possibility of human-to-human transmission cannot be ruled out, the risk of sustained human-to-human transmission is low."[25]

Public pressure was mounting, illustrated by the fact that some people in China began to note with sarcasm on social media that this new virus appeared to be "very patriotic," infecting people abroad but no longer in Wuhan or anywhere else in China itself, where the government continued to embargo information about the growing epidemic.[26] But the reality on the ground, increasingly evident to many people in Wuhan, was that long lines were starting to form at several hospitals, as people with symptoms of pneumonia wanted to be hospitalized for treatment, and others who were uncertain about their condition wanted diagnostic tests.[27] More people began to leave Wuhan than in similar moments during previous Spring Festival seasons, attempting to escape what began to be perceived as a real emergency.[28] Unable to fully repress discussion of the outbreak in social media, facing mounting evidence the outbreak was becoming epidemic, and realizing that Wuhan's healthcare system was becoming overwhelmed, government agencies from the municipal and provincial levels began to cave in to public pressure.

PRESSURES

The days between January 18 and 23 were the key turning point in the government's and society's response to the emergency. A third delegation of the NHC assembled in Wuhan on January 18. Unlike the previous delegations, this one was called a delegation of "high-level experts," and it was led by Zhong Nanshan, the doctor who became famous as the "SARS hero" for telling the truth during the 2003 outbreak.[29] He mobilized the delegation to Wuhan soon after learning about the family cluster near his hometown in Guangdong province that proved human-to-human transmission. The only female member of the delegation was Li Lanjuan, who became famous for implementing strict quarantines that successfully controlled the SARS outbreak in Zhejiang province and for successfully tracing and containing the H7N9 influenza outbreak there in 2017.[30] Finally, the delegation also included George Gao, the director of the China CDC, and a few others.

On the day after the delegation arrived, January 19, the first cases outside of Wuhan were officially confirmed, one in Guangzhou and two in Beijing, laboratory-confirmed cases in Wuhan almost tripled from 77 to 201 cases, and deaths rose from one to three.[31] That day's public statement from the China CDC was still vague, indicating merely that "the transmission route is not yet fully understood."[32] But that afternoon, a closed-door meeting was convened between the members of the NHC delegation and officials from Wuhan and Hubei province, who concluded, upon verification of the latest epidemiological facts, that human-to-human transmission was indeed taking place and might not be limited to hospital or family settings where individuals are in especially close contact. Consequently, they immediately reported this conclusion to the NHC director in Beijing and began to discuss whether or not to call for a lockdown of Wuhan, as previously proposed by Li Lanjuan. That evening the NHC delegation rushed to Beijing and met with the director of the NHC until the early hours of the morning.[33]

Finally, on the morning of January 20, Premier Li Keqiang convened the first meeting of the State Council after signing the "phase one" deal with the US on the trade war and invited Zhong Nanshan and Li Lanjuan to report on the situation in Wuhan. At that meeting, the State Council decided to include the newly identified novel coronavirus disease in the second highest level (Category B) of infectious diseases, but to adopt highest priority (Category A) prevention and control measures. They also called for the prompt release of epidemic information, deepening international cooperation, and expanding disclosure to the domestic public. That afternoon the NHC held a press conference, with Zhong Nanshan, Li Lanjuan, and other experts giving high-profile interviews to the China Central Television (CCTV), confirming that human-to-human transmission was taking place, reporting that fourteen healthcare workers were already infected, and recommending that people avoid traveling to Wuhan and Wuhan residents avoid traveling out of the city. "This is not an official requirement," explained Zeng Guang, the chief epidemiologist of the China CDC. "This is just a recommendation from our group of experts" since "it is likely there is already early-stage community transmission in Wuhan."[34]

The State Council's call for disclosure of information was directed not only at Wuhan and Hubei province, but toward all local governments throughout China. After all, far more people who left Wuhan in the weeks leading up to the Spring Festival traveled to rural areas in the surrounding provinces than to major cities like Beijing, Shanghai, and Guangzhou, yet the latter (and other countries) were the first to report cases of COVID-19 outside Wuhan.[35] This suggests many other local governments surrounding Hubei might have failed to identify early outbreaks in their jurisdictions. With the change in tone from the central government, however, Chinese mainstream media finally began covering the epidemic, and the sudden public shock seems to have stirred even more people to disregard the recommendation to avoid travel.[36] The number of people leaving Wuhan from January 16 to 19 was higher than usual for similar periods in previous years, but there was an even more noticeable spike in travelers leaving the city from January 20 to 23, as news reports began to show that Wuhan's hospitals were becoming overwhelmed. The phrase "flee Wuhan" went viral in social media, becoming the number one topic trending on the microblog platform Sina Weibo on the morning of January 23, when the lockdown was finally announced.[37]

Upon central government orders, Wuhan effectively shut down all air, rail, and road travel from the city, as well as all nonessential business and all bus, subway, and car traffic within the city. "The lockdown of 11 million people is unprecedented in public health history," stated the WHO representative in China, explaining it went "beyond" the WHO's recommendations, but they still welcomed it as "a very important indication of the commitment to contain the epidemic in the place where it is most concentrated."[38] Despite the unprecedented effort, however, the two days between the central government finally triggering a clear public alarm and implementing the lockdown of Wuhan allowed a million or more people to flee the city, some of them spreading the disease to other regions of the country. There may be various reasons for this two-day interval, which might include an conscious strategy to empty out Wuhan as much as possible prior to its lockdown, as the local healthcare system was already overwhelmed by January 21, illustrated by the fact that the percentage of healthcare workers among confirmed cases rose to 7%.[39]

It may also be the case that the lockdown wasn't already decided on January 20, but the mounting pressure of the following days forced the hand of the central government. After all, once local governments were explicitly ordered to report cases in their jurisdiction, it became clear that the outbreak was already surging into a nationwide epidemic, as twenty-five provinces reported cases by January 23.[40] Between January 20 and 22, additional cases were also confirmed in Thailand and Japan, and the first cases were announced in Hong Kong, Macau, Taiwan, Singapore, South Korea, and the US.[41] All of these cases involved travelers from Wuhan, leading various governments to

issue travel warnings and the WHO to consider announc-
ing a Public Health Emergency of International Concern.[42] Moreover, as information began to spread rapidly
outside China, online servers for "preprints" of scientific
articles prior to peer review and publication in journals
began posting research on the novel coronavirus tracking
the outbreak on January 13 and mathematical models simulating the transmission of the disease on January 19.[43]
The most influential of these early-release articles calcu-
lated the likely number of cases in Wuhan based on the
proportion of infected individuals among international
travelers from the city, leading the WHO itself to conclude that instead of a few hundred cases as officially
reported, Wuhan alone was likely to have 4,000 or more
infected individuals by January 18.[44] In other words, the
internet allowed not only for the spread of information
within China through social media, but also a radical
acceleration in the speed through which scientific findings
were disclosed and circulated worldwide.

But all things considered, it is not quite accurate to
interpret this turning point as a "victory of science over
politics." Rather, the shift in the government's and society's responses to the emergency resulted from various
forces from the bottom up among the masses and from
the top down from high-level experts, party officials, and
the international community, and many of these forces
were interpreted through political and economic perspectives. After all, international pressure also translated into
concern over travel restrictions affecting China's integration with global capitalist networks of production, trade,

and finance, and the lockdown of entire cities would certainly disrupt China's globally integrated production networks and drive a slowdown of economic activity, curbing the prospective and hard-fought gains from the "phase one" deal with the US government on the trade war. Moreover, science also wasn't divorced from politics and profits.[45] The tug-of-war regarding which laboratories were allowed to research the genetic sequence of the novel coronavirus directly impacted the race among scientific teams (and their businesses) for prestigious publications and a share in the market of PCR and antibody tests, which were about to boom within China and the rest of the world.[46] The first laboratories, hospitals, and companies to make advancements in this research, after all, were the most likely to gain the lion's share of contracts for testing equipment and operations, more funding for further research and biomedical equipment manufacturing, and also a head start in the race to test—and patent—antiviral medicines, treatments, and vaccines. The WIV, for example, patented the use of the US company Gilead's antiviral medicine remdesivir as treatment for the novel coronavirus disease on January 21.[47] Just as the lockdown of Wuhan indicates how the Chinese state would surge with an iron fist in response to the epidemic, the simultaneous actions of the globally interconnected scientific and business community also indicated the global spread of COVID-19 would unfold hand-in-hand with a surge in scientific, capitalist, and political competition worldwide.

4 SURGE

After the lockdown of Wuhan, China woke up the next day to a Lunar New Year unlike any other. At last, the epidemic gripped the country's attention, as mainstream media and government spokespeople began to report daily increases of confirmed cases. Within three days of Wuhan's lockdown, all provinces reported cases and declared a state of emergency, except for Tibet. One week after the Spring Festival, January 31, 2020, China already had 9,720 confirmed cases and 213 deaths, and the disease had spread to every province.[1] By that date, ten provinces suspended all passenger transport, sixteen provinces suspended all inter-provincial passenger trains, and multiple cities in twenty-eight provinces suspended all bus routes in efforts to curb the spread of the disease. Elsewhere, passengers needed to apply for travel permits. Various cities in addition to Wuhan imposed increasingly strict public health measures, shutting down all nonessential businesses, allowing only a single person per household to go out for essential supplies each day or two, and installing health screening stations anywhere people were still allowed to move through. China had come to a virtual standstill. But the epidemic continued to surge. By February 7, there were 31,211 confirmed cases and 637 deaths. One week later the numbers climbed to 48,548 cases and 1,381 deaths, and by February 21, cases reached 75,569 and deaths numbered 2,239. Toward the end of the month, the daily number of new cases and deaths was clearly declining, but by February 29 a total of 79,394 cases and 2,838 deaths had been confirmed.[2] The collapse of the healthcare system in Wuhan, the dramatic surge of the disease, and the strength of the government's response were shocking to many, and the whole period was marked by palpable social tension and anxiety.

Social tension and anxiety also began to spread with the disease outside China. During this period, the WHO declared the new coronavirus disease a Public Health Emergency of International Concern (January 30) but demurred on the declaration of a pandemic (until March 11).[3] There were 106 confirmed cases in nineteen countries on January 31, most still linked to travelers from China. But during February, cases began to be identified among people with no travel history or contact with arrivals from China. The number of cases outside China tripled between January 31 and February 9, tripled again by February 19, and then grew more than sixfold by February 29, reaching a total of 6,009 confirmed cases and 86 deaths outside China. These international cases were spread across fifty-three countries, including seventeen where local transmission was taking place without any direct ties to travelers from China. At that time, the worst outbreaks outside China were taking place in South Korea (3,150 cases and 17 deaths), Italy (888 cases and 21 deaths), and Iran (388 cases and 34 deaths).[4] Thus, although the daily number of cases was starting to drop within China, it appeared the rest of the world was facing the beginning of a pandemic.

As human-to-human contagion was now recognized, residents from Wuhan and the surrounding province of Hubei began to be stigmatized in China, and Chinese people (and in many cases, Asians in general) faced similar discrimination abroad. Several countries began to impose travel restrictions on China and evacuate their citizens from Wuhan. Meanwhile, people in China began to discuss who should be blamed for this disaster that fell upon them, some accusing the Huanan Market and those who eat, sell, and smuggle wildlife, others blaming scientists who research bat coronaviruses, or the Wuhan and Hubei governments, or even a biological attack from the US. Outside China too, while many countries, NGOs, and individuals sent aid to China, several others stoked anti-China sentiments, blaming Chinese people for the global health emergency, questioning "human rights violations" in the Chinese government's response, and fearing that the burgeoning pandemic and "draconian" response by the Chinese government might upend the global economy as a whole. In this context, the surge of COVID-19 during February challenged the legitimacy of the Chinese government at home and abroad. The response of the Chinese state, business elites, and society at large, therefore, was shaped by their intersection of interests in maintaining political stability, avoiding economic disruption, and providing for public health security and national pride.

This was accomplished by a massive mobilization of healthcare workers and volunteers to Wuhan and Hubei province; people's willingness to follow local cadre and community volunteers who enforced compliance with the lockdowns and other public health measures throughout China; donations of food, supplies, and PPE; accelerated production of medical equipment; and a boom of biomedical research, diagnostic testing, and celebration of the healthcare workers and high-profile doctors struggling to contain the epidemic. All these efforts were effectively coordinated by the Communist Party leadership across various levels of governance. Considering the social tensions and anxieties that marked this period, these efforts were aimed as much at managing popular emotions as curtailing the spread of the disease. Ultimately, this concurrence of state security and public health interests in China accounts for the effective control of the epidemic. However, how these interests were articulated also reinforces a narrow biomedical understanding of the crisis that entrenches state biosecurity over epidemic prevention. In other words, the peak of COVID-19 in China was not only a turning point in the number of cases and deaths, but also a moment when discussion of the origins of the disease yielded to epidemic control, leading to a recovery that reinforces the underlying factors that give rise to emergent diseases in the first place.

BLAME

"From three days before the quarantine order went into effect through the first two days after the restrictions were imposed, most people in Wuhan were in a state of utter panic. Those were five terrifying days that seemed to last forever; meanwhile, the virus was quickly spreading throughout the city, and even the government appeared as if it was at a loss as to what to do."[5] This is how the novelist Fang Fang characterized the events she observed from her apartment in downtown Wuhan, in a diary she began to keep two days after the lockdown went into effect. Originally posted online, and often facing various degrees of censorship, Fang Fang's diary itself would become a major subject of debate among Chinese people discussing the growing epidemic, the merits and failures in the government's response, and who should be blamed. Admittedly, her characterization of events is very negative. The word *panic* appears seventeen times in her book, and *blame* is mentioned thirty-seven times. In her final entry, Fang asserts that "whoever made mistakes and whoever is responsible, those are the people who should carry this burden."[6]

In the early days that Fang began posting online entries about her observations in the quarantined city, many Chinese people responded quite positively, forwarding her entries to their friends and expressing their shared fears and frustrations. Soon, however, many others also started to accuse Fang of fabricating the negative information she wrote about and to criticize her for emphasizing the negative aspects of China and the government's response. The more people debated whether Fang was a heroine for speaking the truth, or a traitor who collaborated with foreigners to spread fake news and anti-China propaganda, the more her daily posts gained attention. Some entries were allowed to stay online like any normal blog post, while other entries were censored as soon as they were posted. Eventually, Fang had to collaborate with others to post entries on her behalf, setting up new accounts each time an account was shut down by censors for posting her material. As usual, however, people continued to find ways to circulate and read her work, taking screenshots of her entries to share as pictures rather than text or rewriting her entries using various codes that could bypass censorship, even if only temporarily.

But government censorship was not the only challenge Fang faced. Above all, she has been subject to extensive trolling, harassment, and even death threats from common people with strong nationalist sentiments and no government connection.[7] In discussing the deeply emotional responses that people expressed during the surge of the epidemic in China, therefore, it is important to avoid oversimplifications that portray victimized masses completely silenced by the government, or a homogenous nationalist celebration of China's capacity to contain the epidemic. Rather than conventional censorship—deleting materials from websites and simply blocking social media posts—top-down and bottom-up actions create a contested digital terrain of public debate.[8]

In this regard, Fang's diary is a useful starting point for discussion. In the early days of the surge of the epidemic, her entries reflect the widespread concern Chinese people faced about the availability of masks and other essential supplies. The fact that masks are useful for controlling the spread of respiratory diseases is not only well established among Chinese and other East Asian epidemiology and public health governance, but also widely understood among the masses, who experienced the SARS outbreak and must cope with high levels of air pollution across various cities.[9] Moreover, unlike the US and elsewhere, there was clear and consistent orientation by the Chinese government that people should wear masks to curb the disease, and in some places police sometimes enforced mask use and social distancing by flying drones with cameras to find those huddling in groups or walking in public without masks and by using loud speakers to scold transgressors.[10]

However, the speed with which public alarm and the epidemic itself were spreading also led to a severe shortage of masks and other medical equipment throughout the country. Although China is the world's largest producer of masks (from the highest quality N95 respirators, through hospital-grade surgical masks, to more basic face coverings of various sorts), when public alarm over the epidemic took hold of the country, many stores and pharmacies quickly ran out of stock, and long lines formed in shops still selling masks. Since it was the middle of the Spring Festival holiday, most factories were paused, with migrant workers scattered back in the countryside. Thus, especially in Wuhan and other cities with rapidly growing outbreaks, many people panicked when facing difficulties finding good enough, or enough, masks.[11] Yet social media posts and high-profile news articles from the period show people directing their anger primarily at shopkeepers who charged exorbitant prices for masks and other essential supplies during the crisis and at individuals who hoarded more than they needed.[12]

There was also anger directed at some government officials, as medical supplies were being shipped across the country to areas facing the worst outbreaks, but some local governments were caught intercepting shipments.[13] A notable incident involved a Wuhan/Hubei government official's driver, who was filmed leaving the Red Cross warehouse with a box of N95 respirator masks at the peak of the shortage, when not even doctors were able to obtain enough of these masks. The government later issued a statement that the masks were taken with the approval of the Red Cross to be distributed among healthcare volunteers, but many continued to suspect the masks were for personal use by the politician and his family. As people looked into the Hubei Red Cross, it was found prioritizing private hospitals that were not leading efforts against COVID-19.[14]

These disputes were effectively laid to rest during February not only through government control of public debate, but also by its collaboration with the Chinese business sector to ramp up production of masks and other PPE, as well as other medical equipment for diagnosis and treatment of the disease. Such government-imposed price controls, increased production, and effective distribution of masks to the population and medical equipment for laboratories and hospitals are ultimately what undergird the apparently "cultural" practice of widespread mask wearing in China. Moreover, as celebrations of this state and corporate capacity gained space in public debates, little attention was given to the structural problems that led China to be caught unprepared without sufficient equipment even for its hospitals, *despite* its globally unmatched production capacity.

This irony was not mainly because a shortage of masks and other PPE was concerning for the masses, but rather because it became tragic for doctors and other healthcare workers. As discussed previously, the systematic shortage of N95 respirators, surgical masks, and other PPE for healthcare workers was a direct result of the privatization of healthcare in China during recent decades and the pressure for even public hospitals to demonstrate profitable operations.[15] Maintaining stocks of PPE is costly, after all, and only necessary in an emergency. State acquiescence to and even encouragement of profit-seeking in the healthcare sector undermined national preparedness for an epidemic outbreak that was clearly foretold. Then, compounding unpreparedness, government and business interests became entangled problematically once again when hospital administrators and party leaders forbade doctors from requesting mask donations on social media, covering up the increasingly severe shortage, in an attempt to curtail public panic and condemnation of government and business alike.[16] As the catastrophe in the US and elsewhere would soon reveal, this problem is not exclusive to China but a characteristic of global capitalism.[17]

The epidemic became a calamity in Wuhan from late January into February largely because hospitals themselves became part of the problem.[18] Given the shortage of essential supplies, healthcare workers began to get infected, inadvertently transmitting the disease to other patients and colleagues before they could recognize their own infection, and then leaving the hospital short staffed when they had to go into quarantine or be hospitalized themselves for treatment. This not only increased the number of people needing diagnostic tests and treatment, but also reduced the number of staff available to maintain hospital operations, which resulted in increasingly large queues forming as people with symptoms sought diagnosis and treatment. "Don't bother coming to this hospital right now," a doctor would say anonymously on social media. "There will be 100 people in front of you waiting to do the clinical exam, and after that there will be another 100 people ahead of you in line for the CT scan and PCR test." The informal advice was that "if you are not so severe, it is better to just stay at home."[19]

Yet as people grew desperate, fearful they might be infected but lack adequate medical treatment, more and more people continued to flock to the hospitals, huddling in the cold outside before they were allowed to enter, crowding the reception halls and waiting rooms seeking assistance, and clustering in the hallways waiting to be seen by the doctors. In such conditions, someone with a common cold, regular flu, or an unrelated sore throat might not have been infected with COVID-19 upon their arrival at the hospital, but there were very high chances they (and those accompanying them) could become infected by the time they left. Alongside the privatization of healthcare in China, therefore, we must also address the cultural shifts that make both people and governments in China prioritize *hospitals* over more decentralized forms of healthcare, such as community clinics and even family doctors attending patients at home, as had been the predominant model during previous eras.[20] Now, however, public funds, private profits, popular admiration, and great demand all concentrate in hospitals, particularly in the largest, newest, and most expensive and comprehensive ones that are considered to be the "most modern," to the detriment of preventive and primary care.[21] This problem is not exclusive to China, but once again a characteristic of global capitalism.[22]

The way Wuhan's healthcare system became overwhelmed and people's veneration of "modern" doctors, pharmaceuticals, medical devices, and hospitals came together in the popular reaction to Li Wenliang's story. Li, who was among the group of doctors reprimanded by the Wuhan police for "spreading rumors" in the beginning of January, became infected himself a few days later while treating a patient without wearing sufficient PPE. "I was feverish on January 11 and was hospitalized the next day," explained Li in a social media post from January 31. "Back then, the government still insisted that there was no human-to-human transmission, and said none of the medical staff had been infected. I was just confused."[23] Li continued to post on social media from his hospital bed, even sharing a picture of himself receiving artificial ventilation, and as his story circulated, he also gained a significant following online. The day he passed away there was great commotion, as some social media and official news outlets reported his death, but a few hours later his hospital countered that he was in grave condition but still alive. Millions watched a live stream for updates about his condition when his death was finally confirmed in the early hours of February 7.[24] The sadness, anger, and frustration that erupted in that moment remains a marker of the epidemic in China. It triggered an uproar for freedom of speech among intellectuals and the masses, and the central government responded by sending a delegation of the National Supervisory Commission to conduct a "comprehensive investigation."[25]

The public uproar unleashed by Li Wenliang's death was also a key factor driving the Chinese central government to scrutinize and discipline government officials nationwide. The party secretaries for the city of Wuhan and the province of Hubei were dismissed from office on February 13, following earlier dismissals of a government official who fumbled responses to basic questions from a journalist about hospital capacity in Huanggang city, which had the second worst outbreak in Hubei. Across the rest of China, another 654 local officials were reprimanded, reassigned, or even dismissed from office in the following weeks and months, as the central government attempted to regain legitimacy with the masses.[26]

But local-level officials did not always leave such criticism unanswered. The mayor of Wuhan, for example, admitted in a live interview on January 27 (seventeen days before the party secretary, who was his superior, was dismissed from office) that the disclosure of information about the outbreak in Wuhan "was not timely."[27] He went on to explain, however, that "the procedures for disclosure must follow the law" and that "as a local government, we needed authorization before disclosing information we received," which was received only after that fateful day of January 20. In this account, therefore, local government officials were muzzled prior to explicit authorization for disclosure from the central government, which implies the blame shouldn't fall upon local officials alone, but also upon those at higher levels.[28]

Regardless of how one interprets Chinese governance and the "hot potato blame game" between central and local government officials, criticism of those who may have been responsible for the crisis extended far beyond the government. Scientists, particularly those who also share government responsibilities, were also accused of prioritizing their own careers over the well-being of the masses. This was expressed mainly through the concern that some scientists might have withheld important information from the public until they could use that data in high-profile publications, particularly in the leading international journals of biomedicine. On the one hand, it is true that articles written by various scholars and government-affiliated scientists appeared in such publications, including the director of the China CDC George Gao, who coauthored highly influential articles in the *Lancet* and the *New England Journal of Medicine*, published on January 24 and 29 respectively, which documented sixteen cases of infected healthcare workers as early as December and proved human-to-human transmission was already evident at the time.[29] Several other leading scientists from China also published similar articles in these and other high-profile international journals between January 24 and 29, questioning the underreporting of total cases in China during that time.[30] On the other hand, many critiques of these scientists did not focus so much on the fact they were "late" in making such information public, but rather on the fact they were publishing abroad and in English.[31] The Ministry of Science and Technology even issued a formal directive on January 30 that called upon the Chinese scientific community to "publish in the motherland" rather than in international journals, so that this information could be more readily available for combatting the epidemic within China.[32] Evidently, lines between public health and nationalist interests were often blurred in ways that left scientists open to public vitriol and even government rebuke.

While some scientists were being accused of selfishness and disloyalty, however, the government and the nationalist masses also closed rank to defend other scientists when people within China and abroad began to wonder if they may have played a role in the origin of the outbreak in the first place. This suspicion was cultivated by multiple factors, including speculative papers in non–peer reviewed preprints that nonetheless circulated widely through international media and active disinformation campaigns against China and some of its most prominent virologists. Such speculation, rumors, conspiracy theories, and disinformation played a key role in Chinese and international public debate about COVID-19, and so this phenomenon should be carefully scrutinized.[33] A good starting point is January 31, when a group of Indian scholars uploaded a non–peer reviewed preprint of an article suggesting the possibility of "unconventional evolution" in the origins of SARS-CoV-2.[34] In other words, they implied COVID-19 was artificially created in a laboratory. Their poor methodology was subject to immediate criticism by other scientists in the comment section of the preprint depository that hosted it, and an uproar in Chinese and international social media led the authors to withdraw their paper two days after posting it.

Four days later, however, two Chinese scholars uploaded a similar preprint to another online depository, pointing out that Tian Junhua, a scientist working at the Wuhan CDC, admitted to accidents while collecting coronavirus samples from bats that could have led to infection (see chapter 1), and that the Wuhan CDC itself was located about 280 meters away from the Huanan Market and adjacent to the hospital where the first outbreaks of COVID-19 were identified in late 2019.[35] Moreover, the authors also indicated that researchers at the Wuhan Institute of Virology (WIV), 12 kilometers away, were engaged in "gain-of-function" experiments that made bat coronaviruses more infectious to humans.[36] They concluded with "a direct speculation [that] somebody was entangled with the evolution of 2019-nCoV," the novel coronavirus, and that it "probably originated from a laboratory in Wuhan."[37] Their conclusion extrapolates the evidence provided, and the authors were subject to intense criticism in Chinese social media, and so they retracted their file from the depository around ten days later. By that time, however, speculation that the origins of the novel coronavirus might be entangled with biomedical research laboratories in Wuhan had already gained traction within China and globally.

Chinese social media was particularly engaged in this debate, peaking around February 15, when the fact that information about a graduate student alumna named Huang Yanling was missing from the WIV website went viral, driving speculation she may have been the "patient zero" that acquired the infection through a lab accident and was then subject to a cover-up.[38] Already on February 16, a notice on the WIV website dismissed such rumors, and Shi Zhengli and Huang's advisor did so as well in social media posts and interviews with mainstream Chinese media, but Huang herself never provided public assurances that quelled skepticism online.[39] Moreover, that same day the story was picked up by US Senator Tom Cotton, a staunchly anti-China Republican, whose denunciations catapulted conspiracy theories about laboratory-related origins of COVID-19 into a global debate.[40]

Still, it would be incorrect to characterize this purely as international disinformation intended to discredit Chinese science and governance. Since February 2, reports circulated online that a high-profile scholar within China itself criticized the general director of the WIV, Wang Yanyi, as someone who was not sufficiently trained and competent enough to manage such a high-risk research facility, alleging that she was placed in that position through personal connections rather than scholarly and administrative merit.[41] Social media posts attributed to another senior researcher at the WIV also reported accusations that Director Wang "often takes experimental animals out of the lab and sells them at the Huanan market," suggesting she might be the culprit for the epidemic outbreak. These rumors were refuted, but still captured many people's imagination and triggered extensive debate in Chinese social media.[42] Reassuring the public, President Xi Jinping issued additional instructions on February 14 to "incorporate biosafety into the national security system and promote the introduction of a biosafety law as soon as possible."[43] The call effectively amounted to strengthening biosecurity at laboratories researching infectious diseases (like the WIV and Wuhan CDC). By then, Major General Chen Wei, an expert on biological weapons and epidemic prevention, had already arrived in Wuhan to conduct research in the BSL-4 laboratory at the WIV and to reassure the public of its biosecurity as well.[44]

Through a series of interviews, blog posts, and then peer-reviewed journal articles, various scientists dismissed the idea that the novel coronavirus was artificially created in a laboratory, and the joint WHO-China investigation in early 2021 determined that a laboratory accident was "extremely unlikely."[45] There is still a need for further research on the possibility of other research-related incidents,[46] but given the negative impact of rumors, speculation, and disinformation, the State Council, Ministry of Science and Technology, and National Health Commission (NHC) issued another ordinance on March 3, 2020, that any research and publications on the origins, diagnostic testing, and vaccines for the novel coronavirus require prior administrative approval.[47] Unfortunately, this also dampens research and rational debate about the topic. After all, the turmoil of the pandemic and the nationalist fervor that erupted in China, the US, and elsewhere effectively forecloses objective discussion of the topic, as impartial investigations and scientific research became highly politicized.

In such circumstances, Shi Zhengli, Wang Yanyi, George Gao, and other experts in the Chinese scientific community began giving public interviews in China and abroad, not only to provide information to the public, but also to reassure that they are individuals who should be trusted and even respected. China joined the global leadership of research on coronaviruses and epidemic control because of them, after all, which also enabled Chinese companies to rush into the forefront of the global race for pharmaceuticals and vaccines to control the pandemic. Consequently, the confluence of state, bio-medical, and nationalist interests dampens examination of the underlying conditions that give rise to pandemics, assuming instead they are inevitable, and promoting a narrow focus on biomedical measures for epidemic control. This sentiment is encapsulated above all in the manner that healthcare workers, famous doctors and scientists, the medical branch of the People's Liberation Army, and the construction of hospitals became celebrated as the heroes and heroic measures that brought the surge of the epidemic under control.

HEROES

The Chinese Communist Party mobilized its 90 million members to inform the people and enforce public health measures. Down to the village level, grassroots cadres and influential individuals patrolled the streets, and sometimes even blocked roads or dug trenches at the borders between various villages, cities, and provinces. Many neighborhood committees also organized collective deliveries of groceries, particularly for elders living on their own. Meanwhile, after January 20, 2020, public health messaging has also been consistent and clear from the top-down in favor of handwashing, wearing masks, maintaining physical distance and avoiding crowds, quarantining confirmed cases, tracing their contacts, and placing them under isolation. Securing compliance is not simply mandated, however; it is also enabled by the financial capacity of the state. Since the Spring Festival 2020, after all, the government has guaranteed that all testing and treatment for COVID-19 be free of cost to all citizens. And it has been top priority among officials from central to local levels to carefully implement the public health advice of experts from the NHC and other organs. It is not simply a surge of state actions that controlled the epidemic. The state operates through interlinked relations with the globalized capitalist sector in China and its nationalist masses, successfully harnessing these interests for public health management, in glaring contrast with the spectacular failure to contain the epidemic in the US, Europe, Brazil, India, and elsewhere.

Across the spectrum, from social critics disgruntled by Li Wenliang's story to government officials who expressed solemn words of respect about him after he died, everyone agreed that the doctors, nurses, and other healthcare workers on the front lines were the first heroes of the moment. Their dedication to the public good in willingly exposing themselves to care for those who are sick is honorable and praiseworthy. Unfortunately, they can only act *after* an outbreak of epidemic disease is already upon us. Biomedical countermeasures effectively fall under a regime of global health security that assumes emerging infectious diseases are an inevitable threat, so all we can do is build response capacity and make technological improvements in disease surveillance.[48] Or in other words, extend even further the power, profits, and cultural attachments to doctors and the modern biomedical equipment of hospitals and laboratories as the paradigm of public health, even if this continued concentration may also become a driving (rather than limiting) factor in the surge of the epidemic, as happened in Wuhan, northern Italy, and New York City.

This process was embodied most clearly in the construction of two specialized hospitals with 1,000 beds each for the treatment of COVID-19 patients in Wuhan. The first hospital, Huoshenshan, was built and became fully operational in twelve days on February 4. The second, Leishenshan, was built about as quickly and inaugurated merely two days later. 5G live streams of their construction became viral in China, and influencers from senior TV personalities to young internet celebrities brought people's attention to the construction of the hospitals by covering it constantly, giving nicknames to construction machinery, and placing bets on how fast the next stage of construction would be done. At its peak, over 40 million people were watching the live stream to witness China's "race against the epidemic."[49] Upon the completion of each hospital, medical officers from the People's Liberation Army arrived, carrying full cargos of medical equipment for the hospitals, which started to receive patients the very next day. Between January 24 and March 8, 42,600 medical volunteers and military doctors, including 19,000 ICU professionals traveled to Wuhan and surrounding cities in Hubei province.[50] With the urging of party and government officials, many companies and individuals throughout China and the global Chinese diaspora also donated masks, medical equipment, and other resources for their hometowns and severely affected areas. It was a collective and celebratory defiance of the epidemic that still makes almost all Chinese people proud.

Beyond the high-profile cases of the two specialized hospitals, the rapid installation of sixteen makeshift hospitals (*fangcang*, or cabin hospitals, in Chinese) throughout Wuhan in early February was also decisive for the containment of COVID-19 in the city. These were quarantine centers set up in public stadiums, conference centers, and fitness centers where people with more mild cases could be isolated, monitored, and treated with both Western medicine and traditional Chinese medicine (TCM), which are combined in an increasingly effective, albeit commercial and industrial, manner.[51] Their technological capacity included CT scans and PCR tests, but not ventilators, so patients whose symptoms became severe were transferred to the specialized or other standard hospitals in the city. Beyond Wuhan, Beijing resumed use

of its specialized hospital built during the SARS outbreak, and various other cities used hotels and dormito-
ries for similar quarantines during the peak of the
epidemic outbreak in February.

Although there was successful and timely deployment
of public health measures, some people who experienced
this traumatic time in Wuhan have much less positive stories to share about Wuhan's hospitals. In a widely circulated online account, for example, a young man explains
how he was turned away from a hospital even though he
had all the clinical symptoms of COVID-19, but the
shortage of PCR testing kits prevented the hospital from
officially confirming his case and hospitalizing him. He
walked from hospital to hospital, but none would admit
him. After spending a few days at home under the care of
his family, and facing pressure from his boss to return to
work, he was finally able to get tested and confirmed. It
was February 11, and the first cabin hospitals were just
being set up. At first, he felt as if he had been secluded in
an empty gymnasium to die, as there were no doctors or
nurses, no medicine, and no way to wash himself in the
portable toilets installed. As more people began to arrive,
basic needs started being met, and nurses and medical
supplies also started to be deployed. People fought off the
fear, anxiety, and uncertainty of the crisis on the phones
with their families, learned how to sleep with masks on,
and prayed to recover enough to be able to return safely
home.[52] Most of them did, even as the trauma of facing
the first burst of a pandemic and the world's most intense
lockdown also continued to mark them and the rest of

Chinese society. Wuhan was called the "hero city" by none other than President Xi himself, showing that the Communist Party and government did not call themselves heroes, but rather the people of Wuhan who undertook the greatest burdens for containing the epidemic.[53] Later in August 2020, Zhong Nanshan received the country's highest award, the Medal of the Republic, and "Zhang Boli, a traditional Chinese medicine expert who presided over the research of the COVID-19 treatment scheme combining traditional Chinese medicine and Western medicine, Zhang Dingyu, head of Wuhan's designated coronavirus-treating Jinyintan Hospital, and Chen Wei, a military medical scientist who made major achievements in COVID-19-related basic research and development of vaccine and protective medicine" were awarded the title of "People's Heroes."[54]

This way of recognizing national heroes is also a way to frame the crisis as a natural and inevitable problem to be managed through a well-integrated expansion of the state apparatus in partnership with science and technology experts who guide the masses. According to this framework, the government should continue training healthcare workers, building hospitals, and expanding biomedical production and technological capacity, while the masses should continue to comply with expert guidance. Yet this framework also conceals how the crisis is not "natural" but results from the way global capitalism drives the degradation of the environment, rising socioeconomic inequalities, and structural vulnerabilities that give rise to novel infectious diseases in the first place, inhibiting the structural transformations required to replace global capitalist interests with socio-ecological sustainability.

In this deeper understanding of the crisis, the advancement of the state with science and technology needs to account carefully for the manner in which some of its own operations might be counterproductive for the purposes of public health and the common good. This includes more than creating and deploying technologies for biosecurity surveillance, from QR codes that monitor individual's health and can restrict their movement to rapid PCR tests. This also requires attention to the underlying epidemics of diabetes, heart disease, cancer, and other diseases that afflict so many people in China and that have continued to rise—and aggravate the risk of death from COVID-19—alongside the modernization of diets and healthcare. These issues are too complex to be remedied through technocratic management. After all, they involve articulations between the modern state, global capitalism, consumerist and nationalist society, and science and technology. Therefore, China's victory over the COVID-19 epidemic is fraught with tension, reproducing the underlying conditions that give rise to emergent diseases even in its successful measures for epidemic control.

5 VICTORY

The course of the COVID-19 epidemic changed dramatically in March 2020. The disease was effectively controlled in China, while it simultaneously became a global pandemic, spreading at an even faster pace and to a far greater extent than witnessed in China during the two previous months. On March 1, the number of new COVID-19 cases in China dropped to 202 and has remained below that number since then (except for July 2020, January 2021, and now in June 2021, when outbreaks reached a few hundred cases per day). By March 7, 2020, daily cases in China fell to 102, but 3,633 new cases were confirmed elsewhere, including 1,234 in Iran, 483 in South Korea, 778 in Italy, and over 100 in four other European countries.[1] By March 9, eleven of Wuhan's sixteen cabin hospitals were decommissioned, since there were no longer enough patients needing isolation, but Italy declared a nationwide quarantine. On March 19, eight days after the WHO formally declared COVID-19 a pandemic, Europe identified 10,221 new cases in a single day and surpassed the total number of confirmed cases in China (87,108 in the former, and 81,174 in the latter).[2] "The number of confirmed cases worldwide has exceeded 200,000," stated the WHO in its situation report that day. "It took over three months to reach the first 100,000 confirmed cases, and only 12 days to reach the next 100,000."[3] The international spread of the disease continued to accelerate, and by the end of March the US, Italy, and Spain (with 140,640, 101,739, and 85,195 cases respectively) all surpassed China's total number of cases, which plateaued at 82,545.[4]

As the month of April came and went, this shift became even more dramatic. On April 8, the lockdown of Wuhan was lifted, and the last twelve COVID-19 patients in Wuhan were discharged from the hospital on April 26.[5] That whole month, China's total number of COVID-19 cases only increased by 1,828, reaching a cumulative total of 84,373 confirmed cases, and 4,643 deaths. Meanwhile, the rest of the world already reported over 3 million cases, over 1 million in the US alone, and over 1.4 million in Europe, and the total number of deaths outside China reached a total of 213,126.[6] Even more significantly, most new cases in China since mid-March were imported from abroad (except for the local outbreaks mentioned above). And so, as the Chinese people and the government began to celebrate their victory over the disease domestically, they also began to guard against new clusters on China's borders and among international arrivals. Public health and security surveillance continued to intensify in China, quarantines were enforced across various cities for travelers from Wuhan and abroad, and the political significance of it all became a major subject of debate. That spring there were discussions in Chinese social media expressing anxiety that COVID-19 might trigger a "new Boxer Protocol," that is, international demands for reparations.[7] Should people blame China for unleashing this monstrous disease onto the world, or should they thank China for its heroic efforts in containing the outbreak and giving the rest of the world time to prepare? Should other countries "copy China's homework" (follow its example), or beware of its authoritarianism domestically and growing geopolitical influence abroad?

The contrast between China's control over the epidemic domestically and the catastrophic advancement of the disease in Europe, the US, and beyond, set the stage for the international tensions and debates that marked the period. In turn, the geopolitical tensions and economic crises that accompanied the spread of COVID-19 around the world also influenced the manner in which the Chinese state and society characterized their victory and efforts toward recovery at home. In terms of containment, China's case is certainly a victory. But despite the obvious mathematical clarity of case numbers and deaths reported by the WHO that contrast China's success with failures abroad, this simple comparison distracts from the systematic problems emerging from global capitalism across China and the rest of the world. Assessment must extend beyond narrow epidemiological framings that overlook the deepening structural factors that foster emergent diseases even in successful measures for epidemic control and economic recovery.

GEOPOLITICS

The day the WHO officially declared COVID-19 a pandemic, March 11, *Foreign Policy* magazine published an article titled "US and China Turn Coronavirus into a Geopolitical Football."[8] Its authors argue, "Beijing is using the outbreak to boost its reputation for global cooperation while Washington plays the blame-Beijing game." Although global relations of power, profits, and public health are not reducible to such interstate competition, this article captures well two of the most important competing narratives during that time. In the discourse emanating from the White House and its political allies, the complex entanglement of state, business, and popular interests that stalled a more effective response to the outbreak in Wuhan boiled down to an oversimplified narrative about the Chinese government's authoritarianism. "Unfortunately rather than using best practices, this outbreak in Wuhan was covered up," the US national security advisor stated, concluding this so-called cover-up "probably cost the world community two months to respond."[9] Yet several other facts identified during this period undermine this interpretation.

Considering cover-ups and inadequate government responses, for example, a whistleblower in the US reported serious security breaches in the US government–run quarantine facilities in California that received US citizens evacuated from Wuhan during February: staff were "not properly trained or equipped" to avoid infection, they weren't tested before they left the quarantine sites, and they traveled to other states without precautions. But upon reporting these failures, the whistleblower was reprimanded and reassigned by their superiors, and both the US Congress and the media stopped following up on the story after March 10.[10] The whistleblower's story may not have been censored, but it was effectively covered up by the increasing outrage regarding far greater problems with the US government's handling of the COVID-19 pandemic that month. In particular, there was a growing uproar about the US government's failure to deploy an effective, extensive, and rapid PCR testing regime, unlike countries such as South Korea and Germany. This was unlikely a mere fluke given Trump's statements that made it evident he was more concerned about keeping the official tally of COVID-19 cases in the US down than curtailing the actual spread of the disease, consistently undermining the advice of his own public health experts and minimizing the risk of the growing pandemic.[11]

These failures of the US government received extensive coverage in Chinese media and circulated widely in social media discussions. After all, the worse things became in the US, Europe, and elsewhere, the more these narratives cast China in a positive light. Regarding the situation in the US, a Chinese social media comment that went viral remarked sarcastically: "No testing, no problem! No problem? So no need for testing! Perfect US logic!" And then once widespread testing finally began and the US surpassed all countries in total number of infections, some Chinese social media users gloated, "Trump was right, US is number one!" Finally, while someone argued the US became "the disaster movie of 2020," another replied "how could it be a disaster movie? Obviously it's a comedy!"[12]

Dark humor is fitting to analyze Trump's behavior. At first he praised China's strong public health measures. "China has been working very hard to contain the Coronavirus," Trump tweeted the day after Wuhan's lockdown and went on to say "the United States greatly appreciates their efforts and transparency. It will all work out well. In particular, on behalf of the American People, I want to thank President Xi!"[13] That was when the US had a single confirmed case of COVID-19, from someone who had traveled from Wuhan. By March 16, however, when the US reached 1,678 confirmed cases and 41 deaths, Trump began to refer to SARS-CoV-2 as the "Chinese virus," in what US commentators immediately recognized as a blatant attempt to "incit[e] a coronavirus culture war to save himself."[14] By that point, US Secretary of State Mike Pompeo had already been using the expression "Wuhan virus" for weeks, the Texas Republican congressman John Cornyn resurrected racist narratives that the coronavirus emerged in China because people there eat snakes (even though some Texans do so as well), and Republican senator Tom Cotton doubled down on the narrative that COVID-19 emerged from a laboratory in Wuhan, even as the US military publicly stated there was no evidence the novel coronavirus was artificially manipulated.[15]

Chinese responses came through a combination of top-down and bottom-up nationalist zeal around equally unfounded accusations that the novel coronavirus emerged instead *in the US*, whether through a laboratory leak or deliberate biological attack against China. On March 12, for example, the spokesman for the Chinese Ministry of Foreign Affairs tweeted that "it might be the US army who brought the epidemic to Wuhan" and demanded from the US government, "Be transparent! Make public your data! US owe us an explanation!"[16] This echoed a rumor that had been circulating in Chinese social media since February that the novel coronavirus was created in a US biological warfare research facility in Fort Detrick, Maryland, which was shut down a few months prior to the US participation in the Military World Games that took place in Wuhan in October 2019. At the event, US soldier-athletes performed poorly and a few returned to the US feeling ill, yet the narrative speculates they still accomplished their mission by deliberately spreading their lab-created disease in Wuhan.[17] Less eccentric theories suggested the novel coronavirus leaked accidentally from Fort Detrick, hence its shutdown in 2019, and COVID-19 was already circulating within the US since late 2019, which accounts for the severity of "influenza" that winter in the US, while the true origin of the pandemic was covered up in the US but detected, and first contained, within China.[18] These accounts, therefore, flip the narrative between China and the US, placing the US in a position of covering up the origins of the new infectious disease, and China as both victim and global hero in the face of the pandemic.

Yet geopolitical disputes are not limited to speculations hurled back and forth between nationalist masses and propagandist politicians of various nationalities. They also include much more respectable scientific issues, such as the WHO's assessment of China's public health measures (including the lockdown of Wuhan), their declaration that the outbreak of atypical pneumonia in China became a Public Health Emergency of International Concern (PHEIC) in January, and the debate in February and early March on whether COVID-19 should be officially classified as a pandemic. The WHO's assessments of the course of the epidemic in China and the Chinese government's response, and its official declarations of a PHEIC and pandemic are intertwined. The first WHO mission to Wuhan took place on January 20–21, and while it reported on January 22 that human-to-human transmission was taking place in Wuhan (two days after the Chinese government first admitted this crucial epidemiological fact as well), the WHO also concluded that "more investigation was needed to understand the full extent of transmission," allowing another week to pass before officially declaring a PHEIC.[19] Of course, there has been an attempt for decades to provide standardized and evidence-based criteria for such definitions, yet the WHO is ultimately a multilateral agency that makes decisions based upon the agreement of its members, who are representatives from state governments. There is a far greater complexity of interests and outcomes at stake in such decisions.

The declaration that an epidemic outbreak has become a PHEIC or pandemic not only recommends that member-states adopt strict public health measures, but also signals to global capitalists (or "markets" as usually discussed in the media) that significant economic disruption is to be expected. When state governments increase public health measures domestically, they also usually impose travel and trade restrictions that stigmatize people and marginalize companies from the epicenter of the burgeoning pandemic. As Andrew Lakoff shows regarding the way the 2014 Ebola outbreak shifted from a "humanitarian crisis affecting a handful of poor countries in West Africa" to an epidemic worthy of designation as a PHEIC, "what changed was not its biological meaning, but rather its political and administrative significance."[20] It shouldn't be surprising the WHO hesitated to declare that COVID-19 was a PHEIC in January, and when it finally did so, it also emphasized that it "does not recommend any travel or trade restriction" and that "countries are cautioned against actions that promote stigma or discrimination."[21]

China's success in containing the disease during February gave the WHO hope a pandemic could still be avoided. The WHO's second mission to China began its investigations on February 16 and issued its report on February 28.[22] The leader of that mission, Bruce Aylward, stated it was still possible to contain the spread of COVID-19 around the world "because we don't have a global pandemic—we have outbreaks occurring globally," and the way to do so was to follow China's example, which he described not only in great technical detail in the official WHO report, but also in various interviews in Chinese and Western outlets alike.

Within China, a post from the official WeChat account of the United Nations went viral on March 4, reporting that "the WHO calls on all countries to 'learn from China' in the process of dealing with such a highly infectious virus that the scientific community knows little about and has no vaccines and therapeutic drugs."[23] The post went on to quote Aylward saying that "in the face of this unprecedented virus, China has adopted 'the bravest, most flexible, and most active prevention and control measures in history.'"[24] On the same day, the *New York Times* also published an extensive interview with Aylward, who stated, "I didn't see anything that suggested manipulation of numbers," dismissing concerns that China's official figures on COVID-19 cases and deaths were repressed by the government.[25] Instead, according to Aylward, "a rapidly escalating outbreak has plateaued, and come down faster than would have been expected. Back of the envelope, it's hundreds of thousands of people in China that did not get COVID-19 because of this aggressive response."[26]

In Aylward's account, this response was aggressive not simply because of the total lockdown of Wuhan and surrounding cities, but also because areas facing just sporadic cases deployed sufficient information and resources to make sure the whole population was washing their hands, wearing masks in public, and avoiding crowds. Moreover, there were health monitoring stations nationwide, rapid deployment of online medical care for non-COVID-19 patients, widespread distribution of food and medications by delivery services, and strong diagnostic capacity. "In the beginning, it was 15 days from getting sick to hospitalization," Aylward admitted, in reference to Wuhan's overwhelmed hospital system. But by the time the WHO's second mission was undertaking its investigation "they got it down to two days from symptoms to isolation," with 200 CT scans being done a day (compared to a dozen or two per day at most Western hospitals), and for the crucial PCR tests that confirm infection by coronavirus, "they got it down to four hours." Moreover, Aylward celebrated the cabin hospitals for isolation of patients with mild symptoms, the construction of the two specialized hospitals, and the remarkable abundance of ventilators and other equipment for critical care. "Its hospitals looked better than some I see here in Switzerland," he indicated, and some even better equipped than the best in Germany. Finally, the *New York Times* journalist asked if China's response was "only possible because China is an autocracy?" Aylward rejected this characterization, saying people in China are "mobilized, like in a war, and it's fear of the virus that was driving them," not fear of the government. "They really saw themselves as on the front lines of protecting the rest of China. And the world." Ultimately, therefore, if other countries had the "political courage" to replicate China's "counterattack" on COVID-19, the pandemic could be avoided.[27]

But during the period from February to March, "sustained community-level outbreaks" became evident in at least three regions outside of China (South Korea, Iran, and Italy). The situation increasingly satisfied the WHO's technical definition of a pandemic.[28] Yet the WHO hesitated to name it as such. At one point, the director of the WHO Health Emergencies Program argued that a pandemic should only be declared when it appeared all people in the world would likely be exposed to the disease within a defined period of time, a distinct criteria that hadn't been previously used by the WHO.[29] In fact, common definitions of pandemic tend to be far broader, such as "an epidemic occurring worldwide, or over a very wide area, crossing international boundaries and usually affecting a large number of people," which obviously characterized COVID-19 by late February.[30] Politically, however, the situation was less clear. The WHO's second mission to China, after all, concluded even large-scale outbreaks such as Wuhan's could be contained. Yet poor countries facing outbreaks, such as Iran, would only be able to do so through humanitarian assistance, but the WHO feared the declaration of a pandemic would lead the US, Europe, and other wealthy countries to limit international aid, as wealthier countries began to stock up on medical supplies for their own use. Meanwhile, some in the US and Europe may have wanted the WHO to declare a pandemic, particularly those stoking anti-China sentiments and accusing the WHO of reproducing "propaganda" from China.[31] But on the other hand, many state and business interests also feared the restrictions on trade and travel that would likely result from the declaration. And indeed, upon the WHO's declaration, the US government announced it would restrict all travel from Europe (with the exception of the UK at first), and the following day global stock markets faced their worst single-day crash since 1987 and the fastest 20% drop in historical record.[32]

In this regard, the timing of the WHO declaration dovetailed very well with the Chinese government's domestic agenda and international diplomacy efforts. It came the day after President Xi traveled to Wuhan, declaring the epidemic was contained there and thanking the healthcare workers, volunteers, and all people of Wuhan for their heroic sacrifice.[33] It was also followed by a declaration that China would donate an additional $2 billion USD to the WHO for epidemic control abroad.[34] Chinese international medical aid contained exports of PPE, medical equipment, and pharmaceuticals, including traditional Chinese medicine (TCM) used to treat COVID-19, and even the deployment of medical teams that integrated Western and Chinese medicine.[35] Later it incorporated development aid and export of vaccines.[36] So that March, while the US and Europe were announcing the closure of borders and international travel restrictions, the Chinese government seized the moment to argue, in a widely publicized letter to the UN, that "public health emergencies are a common challenge to all countries" and thanked "all the countries and international organizations who have provided us with in-kind assistance," before pivoting to the conclusion that "we are now providing medical supplies including testing kits, face masks and preventive gear to several countries affected by the epidemic."[37] In other words, the pandemic was transformed from a domestic crisis in China to an opportunity for international leadership.

RECOVERIES

On March 7, a poem by a staff writer from the Guangzhou-based *South Wind Magazine* went viral in Chinese social media. It was titled "Thank you, Wuhan people!" The poem was accompanied by beautiful pictures of the cherry blossoms that characterize spring in Wuhan, huge light shows projecting the words "Wuhan *jia you!*" ("Come on, Wuhan!") onto the city's buildings and bridges, heroic images of healthcare workers in the hospitals, community volunteers delivering food to residents in quarantine, construction workers eating box lunches after completion of the specialized hospitals, and images juxtaposing the city's now-empty streets with its usual vibrant life before the epidemic. A particularly touching excerpt can be translated as this:

> The virus rages ruthlessly, but the epidemic will go away, and human values will never fade / Illness brings pain, despair, and powerlessness without mercy / Optimism and perseverance are the medicine to break this darkness / This winter is too long / The land of *Jingchu* will eventually come

back from spring / Cherry blossoms are already in full bloom / Peach blossoms are also rustling / In the days ahead to spring / Thank you, people from Wuhan / Thank you for your persistence, the people of this city who have never given up.

The poem brought many to tears. A mixture of sorrow and defiance. A shared pain among Chinese people, recognizing the ordeal that those in Wuhan above all had been going through. The restrictions of the city would only start being eased two weeks later, on March 23, when people from residential compounds deemed to be free of infection could finally start to venture out (as long as their QR health code was "green"), and the lockdown itself would be lifted only two weeks later on April 8. During this time, the feeling of defiance began to outgrow fear and sorrow, and the victory narrative began to take shape.

March 10 and 11 were a particularly important turning point. This was the moment of President Xi's high-profile visit to Wuhan and the official recognition of the pandemic abroad. On March 11, the nationalist newspaper *Global Times* published a headline: "This day has arrived! Beijing found imported cases [of COVID-19] from the United States."[38] The article gloated that there were only six new cases confirmed in Beijing that day, all of them among international arrivals, and one of them from the US, almost evoking a feeling of revenge, given that many Chinese people had felt somewhat ashamed that this disease originated among them and enraged that the US and other countries imposed restrictions on travelers from China. Chinese people faced an intensified racist backlash not only from the statements of politicians like Trump, but also from countless nameless masses in the US and around the world. But this narrative was not simply government discourse, nor simply a response to the growing pandemic abroad. Among Chinese people, the feeling of victory was consolidated by celebration of recoveries and a regained sense of security.

During those same two days, a popular sentiment that the epidemic was being brought under control in China was palpable in the grassroots voices that made various milestones go viral in social media. "60,000 patients have recovered and been discharged from hospitals across all 31 provinces," celebrated a digital poster. "6 days with 0 new cases in Hubei province," indicated another, referring to numbers that did not include the city of Wuhan. "All 16 cabin hospitals decommissioned," indicated another post, making a pun between the words "cabin" and "ark" to call them "the Arks of Life that decisively defeated the epidemic!" Thus, "94 teams with over 8,000 healthcare professional volunteers" who came to supplement Hubei's healthcare system "completed their mission!" These were the main themes that restored a sentiment of hope and pride among Chinese people.

But the sense of victory and security was not shared evenly across all Chinese people. As the pandemic shifted to Europe and the US, Chinese people abroad, particularly international students, felt excluded by their country when strict travel restrictions were imposed by the Chinese government. Starting on March 28, not only were all foreigners banned from traveling to China, but also all airline companies were restricted to a single route per country each week. This effectively stranded tens of thousands of Chinese in the diaspora abroad, right after universities and businesses were shutting down in other countries. As the diaspora became increasingly disgruntled, struggling to return to share in the safety of their homeland, Chinese consulates began distributing masks and TCM through its business and student associations abroad and organized webinars with Chinese doctors about how to deal with COVID-19 abroad.

The new security system based on QR health codes also provides some with a sense of security, while creating privacy concerns and marginalizing others. Individuals are only allowed to move through cities and between provinces when their QR health code is "green," but there was no clear information about what data is utilized in making these assessments, or how and why someone's code might be switched to "yellow" or "red," which restricts that person's movements and forces them into self-isolation at home for a week or institutional quarantine for two weeks.[39] The majority of people in cities using QR health codes, or who travel between cities and provinces, may have faced some frustrations due to technical glitches when the system was being created, but they quickly adapted and don't express much concern about it now. Rather, it appears to be welcomed and even celebrated as part of the modern science and technology that China has developed to successfully deal with the epidemic. But others express concerns about privacy, the possibility these instruments may be used to suppress political dissent, and how such technological requirements further marginalize the poor, rural, and elderly from the benefits of modern society.[40]

Above all, economic inequality shapes the uneven sentiments within China about its victory over COVID-19. The lockdown of Wuhan would continue for another month after the turning point of early March, and it was only lifted slowly and gradually, just as in other cities and provinces, so the long period of strict public health measures caused extensive disruption to China's economy. According to official figures of China's economic performance during the first quarter of 2020, industrial output fell 13.5%, fixed asset investment fell 24.5%, private sector investment fell 26.4%, and retail sales shrank 20.5%.[41] The broad peasant economy was struggling, as many pigs and chickens were culled when supply chains were disrupted and produce couldn't make its way to markets as easily. Those working with wildlife were left in a legal limbo. In the cities, food prices had soared, and countless small and medium businesses went bankrupt. The government would eventually announce support for these small and medium companies on March 30. But with the global economy entering into a downward spiral just as China began to restart its own industries, many export-oriented factories did not hire back many of their workers, and rising unemployment became a real concern.[42]

Therefore, China's challenge became threefold. First, ensure the recovery of those who were infected. Second, foster national pride, popular trust, and international legitimacy. Third, recover its economy while the rest of the world fell into crisis, extending the need for surveillance and containment of the disease.

In efforts to regain the trust of the masses and legitimacy among the international community, various investigations launched by the central government earlier in the year led to noteworthy conclusions in April. First, the government admitted it had been a mistake to crack down on Li Wenliang in early January and honored him, alongside other health professionals, as "martyrs" on April 4, during the Tomb-Sweeping Festival, when people pay homage to their ancestors and mourn the passing of loved ones. This brought closure to the Li Wenliang affair. Then on April 17, the new party secretary in Wuhan revised upward the official numbers for COVID-19 in the city, adding 325 cases and 1,290 deaths to its total tally. The government explained that these errors occurred when hospitals were overwhelmed during the onset of the epidemic in Wuhan, causing some records to contain inaccuracies, and leaving some people to die at home. Also, as China intensified surveillance of international arrivals, it began to document an increasingly large proportion of positive but asymptomatic cases of COVID-19, particularly among younger people. These numbers suggest that COVID-19 was more widespread than initially thought, when only patients with strong enough symptoms were being tested for the disease. In turn, this also suggests official numbers in

China might underestimate the total number of people who were actually infected with COVID-19.[43]

Studies by the WHO and various teams of Chinese and international collaborators estimate that by February 20, 2020, there might have been "232,000 . . . confirmed cases in China as opposed to the 55,508 confirmed cases reported."[44] Another team also estimated that the actual number of COVID-19 infections in Wuhan alone was likely between 204,783 and 320,145 by March 8, 2020, and would have reached 1 million if isolation of patients with mild symptoms had not taken place in the cabin hospitals.[45] The likely undercount of asymptomatic infections at the early stage is not an exclusive problem in China, nor is it the result of a government effort to suppress information. And even if the numbers are three or four times higher than official figures, China was still able to contain the epidemic and had a small fraction of the number of cases in the US, EU, Brazil, India, and Russia. As this fact becomes increasingly evident to people all around the world, the Chinese people's sense of pride, trust in the government, and the international legitimacy of the Chinese state has been not only restored, but even enhanced.

China's ongoing challenge is the dilemma of restarting its economy while maintaining strict public health surveillance, travel restrictions, and sporadic containment measures. This has taken place through ramped up consumerism in Chinese society and the doubling down on capitalist investments, especially for biomedical science and technology, as the way to address the pandemic. In a way, boosting consumerism and domestic investments are necessary given China's position in the global capitalist economy. After four decades of export-oriented industrialization, China found itself trying to reboot its industries while international markets were coming to a standstill. Moreover, people and products from Wuhan and the surrounding Hubei province suffered discrimination, leaving the country's region that suffered the longest shut-down of economic activity also struggling the most to regain access to markets.

The solution was a top-down and bottom-up effort to encourage investment and consumption domestically, beginning with Wuhan itself. Since its reopening, various government agencies and state-owned companies have intensified investments in Wuhan and Hubei province to boost their recovery. On July 16, 2020, the Wuhan city government circulated a series of digital posters marking 100 days since reopening, illustrating its public health and economic recovery and claiming "nothing can stop Wuhan from taking back the time that was lost."[46] On August 12, at a gathering of entrepreneurs in Wuhan, the chairman of one of China's leading agribusiness corporations stated, "Wuhan's post-epidemic revival provided a path for the recovery of the world economy and is of demonstrative significance to the world."[47] Then on August 17, the Wuhan city government reported that almost 17 billion USD in investments were announced for the city's recovery. A significant portion of this included investments in medical care, biomedical research, and the pharmaceutical sector, which were ramping up production of biomedical equipment for research and treatment, including the use of TCM, and making strides in the global race for a vaccine.[48] Meanwhile, mainstream media and social media platforms organized live events to promote "collective buying" through e-commerce from Wuhan, Hubei, and then a rotation of other provinces, which reignited local economies and consumption across Chinese society. E-commerce deliveries and revenues in 2020 increased by 31% and 17% respectively in comparison with the previous year.[49]

The advancement of surveillance technology and the overlap of consumerism with renewed investments and faith in modern science and technology are the key features that characterize China's victory over COVID-19 and that drive its recovery. Despite the global economic crisis due to the pandemic, China's GDP still grew at 2.3% in 2020, and at 18.3% year-to-year in the first quarter of 2021.[50] Yet this recovery also reinforces the conditions that give rise to emergent diseases in the first place and that enabled a local outbreak to become a global pandemic. Thus, the persistence of the COVID-19 pandemic is n‑ purely epidemiological question, it also ‑ olitical, economic, and cultural ways of ‑erging infectious diseases and how to ‑s phenomenon.

6 PERSISTENCE

On June 13, 2020, hundreds of officers from China's military police suddenly swarmed the Xinfadi Agricultural Produce Wholesale Market in southern Beijing, shutting it down for inspection and placing over 90,000 individuals in neighboring residential communities under strict lockdown, as the entire district went into "wartime emergency mode."[1] Seven cases of COVID-19 had been identified in Beijing over the two previous days, and six of them had ties to the Xinfadi Market. The joint police-biomedical operation immediately tested 517 workers at the market and identified forty-five positive cases of COVID-19 that weren't (yet) symptomatic. Moreover, forty environmental samples came back positive as well, particularly from cutting boards used to process imported salmon, fueling narratives that the outbreak originated from contaminated food and packaging imported through frozen supply chains, where the coronavirus might be able to survive longer.[2] Through rapid contact tracing and PCR testing, Beijing's total number of new COVID-19 cases increased to 77 the next day and 158 four days later, when additional cases linked to the outbreak in Beijing also started being identified in Hebei, Liaoning, Sichuan, and Zhejiang provinces.[3] Anxin county in Hebei province, which borders Beijing's southern district where the outbreak started, and where many Xinfadi workers reside, placed all its half million residents back under strict lockdown on June 28, allowing only a single person per family to leave their home each day for essential supplies. The outbreak resulted in 311 new cases of COVID-19 in Beijing alone since it was first detected that month.[4]

Prior to the outbreak at the Xinfadi Market, Beijing had recorded fifty-six days without any local transmission (all new cases registered during that period were identified among travelers to the city). The city had just lowered its public health alert ten days prior to the outbreak and was in the midst of reopening its schools. But all schools then reverted to remote instruction, and seven more neighborhoods were placed under lockdown as the whole city returned to its highest level of alert. Xinfadi is no ordinary market but is Beijing's "vegetable basket," the wholesale hegemon that provides about 90% of the capital's fruits and vegetables, including all imports, and a significant amount of its seafood and meat as well. It is fully indoors, air conditioned, and operated by about 10,000 workers, so an outbreak there could certainly trigger a super-spreader event for the whole city, and even reignite a national epidemic.

The outbreak at Beijing's Xinfadi Market shocked the nation, since it was the first serious outbreak of COVID-19 since March that was not linked to international arrivals. Moreover, it took place within the nation's capital itself, and its link to wholesale markets and fresh seafood was reminiscent of the wet markets at the epicenter of Wuhan's outbreak the previous year and in Guangdong during the SARS outbreak many years before. Yet Xinfadi is not a "messy wet market" selling illegal wildlife. It is the most modern wholesale market in the country's capital, renovated as recently as 2017 with the highest standards of food safety and public health. The outbreak was fully contained by July but underscored that the threat of COVID-19 persists in China and that China must persist in its efforts of surveillance, containment, treatment, and investigation of this ongoing pandemic.

Still, the way that Chinese mainstream and social media narratives began to account for this outbreak rarely questioned the wisdom of maintaining such a highly concentrated food supply chain, or the failure of the highest standards of food safety and public health to avoid an outbreak. Instead, almost all discussion focused on the *imported* salmon that may have been the root cause of the outbreak. Salmon was pulled from the shelves of all retail markets in the city, retail was halted in Beijing's six large-scale seafood and meat markets, and the government launched an extensive testing campaign on imported frozen food items and the entire cold supply chain. This shifted the Xinfadi outbreak from comparisons with the

Huanan Market in Wuhan to a comparison with other clusters on China's borders with Central Asia and Russia, major port cities, and international arrivals at China's major airports. In other words, COVID-19 remained an *external* threat to China, something that came from other countries that failed to contain the pandemic.

Moreover, the Xinfadi outbreak also allowed for a reenactment of China's effective epidemic containment measures. It emphasized the strong capacity of the government to deploy science and technology to test and trace new cases, and mobilize state actors and the masses alike to adopt quarantines and lockdowns that can halt a surge of infections and control the epidemic. Finally, it set a forward-looking and ecomodernist framework for what is to be done: scientific investigations of cold supply chains and development of technological improvements to prevent infection from imported frozen foods, enabling the persistence of China's connections with global capitalism. However, this framework also forecloses reflection about the underlying political, economic, and ecological conditions of China's food system, including the growing concentration of production, processing, and distribution for the rapidly rising populations of major cities. It also prevents critical evaluation of the broader dynamics of urbanization and environmental degradation that increase the risks of new infectious diseases jumping species. This includes the expansion of infrastructure, mining, wildlife farming, and tourism in peri-urban and remote rural areas, such as the mountainous region of southwest China and Southeast Asia where SARS-like coronaviruses are endemic among bats, and the dramatic rise of e-commerce that is becoming one of China's hallmark contributions to global capitalism.

The persistence of the COVID-19 pandemic, therefore, and how China's victory over the disease frames its measures for epidemic control through uncritical faith in science, technology, and capitalist modernization brings us back full circle to a deeper discussion of the conditions that give rise to emerging infectious diseases, including the various intermediaries and exposures that characterize this process, and the entanglements of the Chinese state with global capitalism and the nationalist, consumerist, and ecomodernist culture of its society.

ENTANGLEMENTS

The Chinese government's approach to public health clearly enabled a much more effective containment of the initial epidemic within China and of subsequent clusters that continue to flare up as well. This is particularly evident when compared with the catastrophes still unfolding in the US, Brazil, and India, for instance. But it is clear that both the emergence of this novel coronavirus and the rapid expansion of a local outbreak into a global pandemic require us to examine China in a much broader perspective, particularly its articulations with global capitalism, and the complex configuration of nationalism, consumerism, and ecomodernist trust in biomedical sciences and technology that characterize contemporary Chinese society. Ultimately, these entanglements characterize the way the Chinese government and society frame the narrative about the victory over COVID-19, efforts at recovery from the epidemic, and the unfolding global economic crisis. But rather than preventing similar pandemics in the future, there are troubling signs that we may be moving in the opposite direction.

"We have entered a new pandemic era, one in which epidemic and pandemic emergences are becoming commonplace," concludes a study on the origin of COVID-19 by an interdisciplinary team from the US and Australia.[5] "Understanding how COVID-19 emerged is a critical point on a steep learning curve we must quickly master," they continue, "as we face the mounting deaths and societal upheavals of the COVID-19 pandemic, we must not lose sight of how this pandemic began, how and why we missed the warning signs, and what we can do to prevent it from happening again—and again."[6] The rapidly increasing incidence of emerging infectious diseases is well known, and the specific risk of bat coronavirus–linked diseases emerging in China was widely reported among the scientific community from at least 2005 until as recently as 2019.[7] Yet despite all the advancements in virology, epidemiology, environmental sciences, and biosecurity, a "monster" that was known to be standing "at our door" barged in with a roar (to borrow Mike Davis's expressions). Evidently, when state, capitalist, and popular interests effectively merge into a coordinated effort, as in China, it is possible to contain an epidemic outbreak. The record-speed development and deployment of multiple vaccines for COVID-19 is likely to control the pandemic, even if the disease never becomes eradicated but continues to circulate endemically like seasonal influenza. Thus, as observed by that interdisciplinary team studying the origins of COVID-19, "our science is sufficiently robust to have a good chance of controlling pandemic viral emergences within 2–3 years, but dramatically insufficient to prevent and control their emergences in the first place."[8]

This conclusion usually leads to the interpretation, within China and most of the international scientific community alike, that pandemic emerging diseases are inevitable, so we must intensify our efforts to improve biomedical science and technology for epidemic disease *control*. Thus, pandemics are framed primarily in terms of *biosecurity*, connecting improvements in biomedical surveillance and public health management of populations domestically, with the right mix of humanitarian biomedicine and international biosecurity cooperation. In other words, the purpose becomes the continued cultivation of global health regimes of "preparedness" for presumably inevitable pandemics.[9] This framework for "preparing" the country and the world for epidemic outbreaks emerged when new varieties of influenza with pandemic potential were recognized in southern China during the 1990s, became consolidated in the aftermath of the SARS outbreak, and now is advancing even further with the COVID-19 pandemic.

This international framework may be recent, but it isn't a simple foreign imposition of globalization upon China. Rather, it became hegemonic in China through deep-seated connections between state-making, biomedical sciences, and the particular cultural characteristics of Chinese society. Historians of public health in China demonstrate, for example, that "Chinese elites [have] accepted a medicalized view of their country's problems and embraced a medicalized solution for the deficiencies of both the Chinese state and the Chinese body" since the colonial encounters of the late nineteenth and early twentieth centuries.[10] Ancient Chinese notions of medicine became increasingly reframed in terms of *weisheng*, which translates not merely as "hygiene," but even more meaningfully as "hygienic modernity."[11] During the Maoist era, this struggle unfolded through political campaigns that directed scientists to eradicate polio and smallpox through mass vaccination, and that enrolled the masses to eradicate rats, flies, mosquitoes, and other animals that carry diseases, including parasites that cause snail fever (*schistosomiasis*), and even agricultural pests through nonchemical/non-pharmaceutical interventions.[12] Despite radical political differences between the late Qing empire, republican era China, and the revolutionary campaigns of the Maoist era, it is possible to trace a continuous process of state-making through the deployment of public health measures, which enables increasingly stronger state surveillance of Chinese society, increasingly more interlinked relations between the government and biomedical sciences, and a paradoxical culture that celebrates Chinese nationalism on the one hand, and "superior" science and technology from abroad on the other. Since the market-oriented reform of the 1980s, this paradoxical relationship with foreign science and technology has become increasingly structured by global capitalism, while state-making through public health measures is perceived as a supposedly apolitical instrument of modern technocratic management. As discourses of public health and modernity become increasingly intertwined, the Chinese state and society see themselves now transitioning from mere recipients of modern medicine to partners or even leaders in the advancement of a global regime of health security, undergirded by profitable biomedical science and technology, including promotion of the integration of traditional Chinese medicine (TCM) with Western medicine.[13] But while this process advances China's position in the global health security regime, it also harbors tensions that might perpetuate the emergence of infectious diseases with pandemic potential.

Consider how the Chinese mainstream conceives of "prevention" in the aftermath of COVID-19, characterized by the ban on wildlife trade, crackdown on wet markets, and reinforcement of virus-hunting and human health surveillance. The ban on wildlife consumption and trade is designed to target specifically those animals consumed primarily as luxury food items, leaving out species that are considered to be of use for TCM and those that can be incorporated into agroindustrial production practices. The Chinese Academy of Forestry, the state-sponsored research institution that is primarily responsible for wildlife management, continues to "strongly propose captive breeding as being the only feasible approach to China's wildlife conservation–utilization dilemma" and frames critique of this approach as a "negative international attitude toward China's attempts to rationalize the utilization of wildlife."[14] Even prominent Chinese scientists with strong international ties, such as Wang Linfa (director of the Programme in Emerging Infectious Diseases at Duke-NUS Medical School in Singapore and member of multiple WHO committees on COVID-19) are unable to think beyond this narrow eco-modernist approach.

At a recent webinar on COVID-19 and other emerging bat-borne diseases, for example, Wang stated that prevention ultimately requires that "we have to protect [bats'] natural habitat" and limit "risk factors, for example, bat colonies [that] are too close to pangolins or civet farming."[15] Hardly anyone disputes this fact, but *how to undertake such environmental protection* remains a subject of intense debate. In Wang's view, "we have to ban, or at least, really regulate wildlife farming and trading in a much more biosecure, biosafe environment, *just like we do for chicken farming and pig farming*."[16] Evidently, Wang's expertise in zoonosis and emerging infectious diseases is derived from his training in molecular biology, not political ecology and critical agrarian studies. After all, setting the highly industrialized chicken and pork industries as an example for emerging disease *prevention* is deeply shocking, if not outright laughable, given how the year-round concentration of livestock with extremely limited genetic diversity and extremely confined conditions is the perfect recipe for the production of highly pathogenic viruses with pandemic potential, as widely acknowledged in the literature on zoonotic and emerging diseases.[17]

An alternative paradigm that can reduce the risk of infectious disease spillover from animals much more effectively would not replicate the "modern" features of the poultry and pork industry for wildlife farming, but rather dismantle those unsustainable agroindustries themselves, and de-concentrate both animals and humans from urban metropolises. A less concentrated and more sustainable agrifood system, based upon agroecology rather than pesticides, genetic engineering, and pharmaceutical therapies for disease-prone concentrated livestock, would actually curtail human encroachment into relatively undisturbed wilderness areas. This argument appears to contradict mainstream opinions, but it is substantiated by the International Assessment of Agricultural Knowledge, Science and Technology for Development (IAASTD), a project cosponsored by the United Nations' Food and Agriculture Organization (FAO) and Global Environment Facility (GEF), the UN Development Programme (UNDP), the UN Environment Programme (UNEP), the UN Educational, Scientific and Cultural Organization (UNESCO), the World Bank, and the WHO, which included input from over 900 scientists worldwide and has China and 109 other countries as signatories.[18] Moreover, a recent report by the UNEP on pandemic prevention, written in response to COVID-19, explicitly rejects the ecomodernist strategy of reducing the risk of zoonosis through further integration of wildlife into agro-industrial production chains.[19] "In theory, wildlife farms could provide proper sanitary conditions that reduce the risk of disease transmission. But in reality, the risk of disease transmission with wildlife farms is significant," states the UNEP.[20] Institutionalizing and intensifying the farming of wildlife can actually increase consumption and demand for wildlife products, enable illegally poached wildlife to be "laundered" as though they were farmed, increase the close contact between humans and different species of wildlife and domesticated animals, and thereby "trigger emerging disease events with higher pandemic potential because these viruses are more likely to amplify via human-to-human transmission, and thus spread widely."[21] Ultimately, "any significant increase in the farming of wild animals risks 'recapitulating' the increases in zoonoses that likely accompanied the first domestication of animals in the Neolithic era, some 12,000 years ago."[22]

The same contradictions are seen in the ecomodernist alliance between the Chinese state, society, and global capitalism regarding the modernization of wholesale agrifood markets and surveillance of novel viruses and human health. China has embarked on a campaign to "upgrade" its wet markets, modernizing them according to the latest global standards of food safety and public health. Illustratively, in June 2020, the World Bank awarded a 300-million

USD loan for the governments of Hainan and Jiangxi provinces to build institutional capacity based on "international good practices" of risk-based surveillance, wet market management, and animal husbandry.[23] This includes "defining a new balance between protection and reasonable use of certain species" of wildlife, developing "farm-specific disease management plans," "deploying digital technologies for better animal disease and food safety surveillance," and "piloting 'healthy marketplaces' practices through upgrade of local wet markets."[24] In other words, increasing state capacity to modernize wildlife farming and wet markets according to the standards of global capitalism.

Once again, the UNEP provides a much more skeptical opinion about the capacity of such initiatives to prevent pandemics. "Expert opinions differ as to whether live animal markets should be regulated more strictly, gradually upgraded with buy-in from vendors, or banned completely in order to reduce disease transmission risk," the UNEP reports, and emphasizes that "food from modern retail outlets is not always safer than that from informal markets."[25] To illustrate this point, the UNEP points out that "there have been many outbreaks of COVID-19 from the massive, crowded, artificially chilled industrial meat plants in Europe and America, but much fewer from smaller, naturally ventilated meat plants in many low- and middle-income countries. Thus, it cannot always be assumed that the modernization of food value chains will reduce risk."[26] And within China itself, as noted in the opening of this chapter, the first domestic outbreak of COVID-19 since the first surge of the epidemic was centered in Xinfadi, one of the most modern and well-regulated wholesale markets in Beijing.

Surveillance of viruses and human populations for early detection of an epidemic outbreak is another point where the same ecomodernist tensions come to the foreground. The risks and benefits of virus-hunting expeditions need to be subject to far more nuanced analysis and public debate. Yet the Chinese government, scientific establishment, and nationalist society are shielding Chinese scientists and research institutes involved in this work from scrutiny. This isn't an exclusive problem of China alone, as such practices are also common among the international scientific community, who place such high-risk surveillance practices as a cornerstone of "One Health" approaches to pandemic prevention. The most notable of these initiatives is doubtlessly the US government–funded PREDICT project, which received over 200 million USD since 2009 to collect over 140,000 biological samples from animals all around the world, including 10,000 samples from bats. The project identified over 1,200 viruses with pandemic potential, including 160 new strains of coronavirus.[27] Despite its name, the project was unable to *predict* the emergence of COVID-19, and this cannot be simplistically reduced to the project's recent termination by the Trump administration.

Containment of the surging epidemic in China was much more clearly the result of early twentieth century public health techniques—such as mass mobilization for isolation and quarantine, handwashing, and masking—

than a consequence of discoveries by the PREDICT program and other similar international projects, such as the efforts of the EcoHealth Alliance and the Global Virome Project. Consider the genetic sequencing of viruses and PCR tests, for example. They do enable greater confidence in the diagnosis of infectious diseases. Yet limiting official confirmation of COVID-19 cases to those individuals with positive PCR test results was also a major problem during the surge of the epidemic in Wuhan and the US alike. Doctors sometimes had complete confidence that a patient was infected with the novel coronavirus due to their experience with clinical diagnostics (including CT scans in the case of Wuhan), but could not officially declare the individual a "confirmed" case and admit them into quarantine at the hospital because they did not have enough PCR testing capacity. Consequently, countless individuals were turned back to their homes, spreading the disease further while they remained merely "suspected" cases in official records.[28] Such dependence upon PCR tests was even more catastrophic in the US, where testing was fumbled longer than in any other major country, but clinical diagnostics were not utilized to isolate individuals who were likely to be infected with COVID-19. It is not clear, therefore, that virus-hunting to accelerate the genetic sequencing of viruses and their identification through PCR testing was essential for the containment of COVID-19 outbreaks.

Considering in addition the highly contentious practice of many among these scientists to persist in undertaking "gain-of-function" experiments that increase the capacity of viruses to infect humans (in order to better understand how they might evolve to cause a pandemic), we must question much more forcefully if the risks associated with this research outweigh its supposed benefits.[29] Once again, this is not a critique of the Chinese scientific community, government, or society, but rather a critique of the ecomodernism that sustains such practices in the name of pandemic prevention, while increasing the risks they seek to curtail. And within China itself, there are also powerful voices expressing such concern. Du Qun, vice president of the Environmental and Resource Law Research Association of the Chinese Law Society and director of the Centers for Environmental and Resource Law and Economic Law at the Beijing University of Aeronautics and Astronautics, said in an interview with the *Beijing News* during the peak of China's COVID-19 epidemic: "There should be principled regulations for restrictions on biotechnology. In such emerging fields, scientists have the instinct to explore the unknown, but they should also follow the ethical principles of scientific research and bear the social responsibility of ensuring harmlessness. They should not lead science to disorder, get lost in the labyrinth of technology, and put humanity in a dangerous situation."[30] Yet it appears that if China persists on the global path of virus-hunting expeditions, gain-of-function experiments, and glorification of biomedical sciences to the detriment even of clinical diagnosis and public health, the risks will continue to increase that China may be at the epicenter of another pandemic.

Ultimately, China seeks to lead the world not only in biosecurity, but also in the economic recovery from the crisis triggered by COVID-19. This includes promoting 5G Wi-Fi networks, and the technologies for digital surveillance it enables, and the provision of biomedical equipment ranging from simple surgical masks and PCR test kits to costly ventilator machines, pharmaceutical drugs, including TCM, and, of course, the holy grail of effective vaccines. But neither the improvement of digital technologies nor China's unmatched industrial capacity mean that modernizing and restocking global biomedical supplies will enable the world to be any better "prepared" for a future pandemic.[31] Ultimately, this form of recovery through ecomodernism consolidates an unsustainable and unjust development paradigm that entangles China even more with global capitalism. This extends even to the commodification of TCM, which creates various tensions: between the need for natural ingredients and the destruction and contamination of the environment that makes it increasingly harder to produce traditional medicines, between the ideal of affordable healthcare and the growing need to turn profits, and between the philosophical notion that health results from particular environmental and specific bodily conditions and the pressure to scale-up, industrialize, and universalize TCM pharmaceuticals.[32] The integration of TCM with Western medicine is helpful to treat patients more holistically and with fewer side effects, but it also advances the capitalist transformation of TCM.[33] Between 2017 and 2020, TCM revenues increased 71% to 434 billion USD, the fastest growing category being pharmaceuticals.[34]

Global capitalist practices of commodifying health-care; industrializing agriculture and livestock; expanding mining, infrastructures, and tourism into remote regions; sacrificing nature for profit; and promoting consumerism among increasingly urbanized people suffering more and more chronic health conditions increase the risk of animal-borne viruses spilling over into humans and triggering catastrophic pandemics. Instead of enabling the de-concentration of people from metropolitan regions and providing preventive health care at the village and local community levels, persisting in this paradigm deepens the cultural and economic drivers that bring people from remote regions (where they may be exposed to new diseases from wildlife) into densely interconnected global cities and crams sick people into a few major hospitals. Instead of cultivating a new approach to science, technology, and political economy that places human health and well-being as their purpose, persisting in this paradigm deepens the entanglement of science and technology with profit interests, enabling consumerism for the masses and perpetuating wealth for global capitalist elites. The persistence of COVID-19 will continue to drive geopolitical struggles and competition over the power and profits generated by biomedical science, and the persistence of global capitalism in China will continue to drive the emergence of infectious diseases with pandemic potential. To alter this course we must replace geopolitical competition and blame games with internationalist cooperation, restructure healthcare away from private profit and toward the common good, and transform our understanding of pandemics from narrow technocratic and biomedical frameworks to encompass the complex entanglements of political, economic, ecological, and social factors at play.

China continued to detect a few dozen new cases of COVID-19 each day through late 2020, mostly linked to international arrivals, until a cluster in Hebei province (near Beijing) in January 2021 demonstrated limited community transmission in a peri-urban area near Shijiazhuang's international airport. This renewed local lockdowns and national precautions, and the outbreak was quickly contained through rapid CT scans and PCR testing, contact tracing, the relocation of entire communities to isolation, and copious use of Western and traditional Chinese medicine treatments. The outbreak was swiftly contained but reminded China that it must stand guard against the continued threat of the pandemic. Meanwhile, the US, Europe, and other countries faced the largest surge yet during that winter. By mid-June 2021, the WHO reported over 173 million cases worldwide and over 3.8 million deaths from COVID-19, including 33.2 million cases and about 600,000 deaths in the US alone, and the rest concentrated mainly in Europe,

India, and Brazil. Meanwhile China's totals since its first outbreak only reached about 116,665 cases and 5,306 deaths. While some westerners resurrected the century-old trope of China as the "Sick Man of Asia" at the beginning of the epidemic, the tables have since turned and now the US is cast instead as "Sick Uncle Sam."[1] Chinese people celebrated the Spring Festival in 2021 under a "remain in place" policy, and multiple negative PCR tests and green QR health codes are required for travel. China's persistent public health measures continue to work but still carry the tensions and dilemmas of modernization and global capitalism.

Looking back, the joint WHO-China investigation of the origins of the pandemic in Wuhan identified four hypotheses. They conclude a "laboratory incident [is] extremely unlikely" but did not explicitly rule out other research-related incidents, such as the possibility of an accident during a virus hunting expedition, which would be a possible instance of a second hypothesis, a "possible to likely pathway" of direct exposure to the original host of SARS-CoV-2.[2] Direct exposures can occur not only through research, but even more likely through mining, farming, tourism, or other contact with bats that carry SARS-like coronaviruses, not only in China, but also in Thailand, Cambodia, or other countries.[3] The third and leading hypothesis according to the joint WHO-China study (considered to be "likely to very likely") is that intermediary species might be involved, and so they call for further investigation of wild animal and livestock farming, smuggling, transportation, and commercialization, which connect Wuhan to domestic and global commodity chains.[4] Their fourth hypothesis considers that the novel coronavirus may have arrived in Wuhan through the cold supply chain, particularly frozen meat. This hypothesis is emphasized by Chinese actors, since it expands the scope of investigation far beyond China's borders. However, this is not an independent hypothesis of zoonosis, as it can only "reflect direct zoonotic transmission [elsewhere], or spillover through an intermediate host."[5] Although this cold chain hypothesis deflects geopolitical pressure away from China, it also reinforces the critique of modernization and industrialization of food systems, particularly animal husbandry and the long food miles of global agribusiness. So whichever hypothesis turns out to be the case, it is evident that the investigation of the origins of COVID-19 isn't about tracing the pandemic to a "patient zero," "bat zero," "ground zero," a cultural practice, or a specific spillover event—it is ultimately about revealing the structural conditions of global capitalism that give rise to novel infectious diseases with pandemic potential, and exposing the limitations of biomedical approaches and ecomodernist frameworks that conceal the urgent need for agro-ecological and sustainable transformations that cultivate public health and the common good.

Looking forward, China transformed its crisis into an opportunity for national development and international influence. While Trump was quitting the WHO to pursue an "America First" policy and the new Biden administration confronts an uncontrolled epidemic in the US, China sets a good example of epidemic control internationally and increases its soft power through medical aid and exports of masks and vaccines. As a *New York Times* editorial recently put it, "The era of vaccine diplomacy is here."[6] But the global challenge we face is not just about a race between China, the US, Europe, Russia, and emerging economies like India for public health, biomedical, and economic leadership. The persistence of the pandemic is creating conditions for new variants of SARS-CoV-2 to evolve, mutating ahead of the record-speed development of vaccines and antiviral treatments, thereby undermining their efficacy.[7] Thus, the COVID-19 pandemic advances in parallel with other pandemics of HIV, influenza, tuberculosis, and chronic diseases, especially in the Global South, where public health systems are much more vulnerable and people are more marginalized in the global regime of biosecurity. The current unevenness of public health capacity and cutting-edge vaccines may transform COVIDs into globally endemic diseases, as the rising dominance of a more contagious variant of SARS-CoV-2 in the UK, South Africa, Brazil, and India foreshadows. So beyond racist scapegoating and simplistic comparisons or blame games between China, the US, and other countries—which hinder international collaborations for investigating the origins of COVID-19 more objectively—this pandemic teaches us that global public health is not derived from the "most modern" countries and biomedical practices, or even the "most effective governance strategies," but rather from our capacity to transcend global capitalism in the interest of socio-ecological justice, sustainability, and the shared destiny of humanity.

ACKNOWLEDGMENTS

First, special thanks to my husband, Gustavo Oliveira, for accompanying me as my life partner and colleague, stimulating me intellectually, polishing my manuscripts, and supporting me emotionally during this pandemic. This gratitude extends also to my family in China and my in-laws, who stayed so close to us even though we could not visit each other, as we all struggle through so many challenges. There are many colleagues and mentors whom I want to thank, including Eve Darian-Smith, Philip McMichael, Robin McNeal, Qi Gubo, Ye Jingzhong, Sun Jin, and others who have supported me along the way. Many thanks as well to the two anonymous peer reviewers, Marcela Maxfield, Sunna Juhn, Catherine Mallon, and the rest of the team at Stanford University Press. Last but not least, I am deeply grateful to all the essential and frontline workers who expose themselves daily to maintain our lives during this extremely difficult time.

NOTES

CHAPTER 1

1. Davis, M. (2006). *The monster at the door: The global threat of avian flu.* New York: Macmillan.

2. Xu, R., et al. (2004). Epidemiologic clues to SARS origin in China. *Emerging Infectious Diseases, 10*(6), 1030–1037; Kleinman, A., & Watson, J. (2006). *SARS in China: Prelude to pandemic?* Stanford, CA: Stanford University Press.

3. Huang, C., et al. (2020). Clinical features of patients infected with 2019 novel coronavirus in Wuhan, China. *Lancet, 395*(10223), 497–506.

4. The WHO data calculates separately the number of cases/deaths in Hong Kong (1,755/299) and Taiwan (346/73).

5. After that first surge, infections only increased gradually to 116,665 cases and 5,306 deaths by June 16, 2021.

6. Davis, *The monster at the door*; Davis, M. (2020). *The monster enters: COVID-19, avian flu and the plagues of capitalism.* New York: OR Books; Wallace, R. (2016). *Big farms make big flu: Dispatches on infectious disease, agribusiness, and the nature of science.* New York: Monthly Review Press; Wallace, R. (2020). *Dead epidemiologists: On the origins of COVID-19.* New York: Monthly Review Press.

7. Davis, *The monster enters*, pp. 16–17. Oldstone, M. (2009). *Viruses, plagues, and history: Past, present, and future.* Oxford: Oxford University Press; Snowden, F. (2019). *Epidemics and society: From the Black Death to the present.* New Haven, CT: Yale University Press.

8. Davis, *The monster enters*, p. 18.

9. Ibid., p. 44.

10. Wallace, *Big farms*, p. 83.

11. Greenhalgh, S. (2020). Governing through science. In S. Greenhalgh & L. Zhang (Eds.), *Can science and technology save China?* Syracuse, NY: Cornell University Press.

12. Schmalzer, S. (2016). *Red revolution, green revolution: Scientific farming in socialist China.* Chicago: University of Chicago Press.

13. Greenhalgh, Governing through science, p. 2.

14. Ibid., p. 3.

15. Ibid., p. 16. See also Mason, K. Divergent trust and dissonant truths in public health science. In *Can science and technology save China?*, pp. 95–114; Lord, E. China's eco-dream and the making of invisibilities in rural-environmental research. In *Can science and technology save China?*, pp. 115–138; Greenhalgh, S. The good scientists and the good multinational. In *Can science and technology save China?*, pp. 139–162.

16. Hu, B., Ge, X., Wang, L., & Shi, Z. (2015). Bat origin of human coronaviruses. *Virology Journal, 12*, 221; Cui, J., Li, F., & Shi, Z. (2019). Origin and evolution of pathogenic coronaviruses. *Nature Reviews Microbiology, 17*(3), 181–192.

17. Ibid.

18. Zhou, P., et al. (2020). A pneumonia outbreak associated with a new coronavirus of probable bat origin. *Nature, 579*(7798), 270–273.

19. See, for example, Cost, B. (2020, January 23). Revolting video shows woman devouring bat amid coronavirus outbreak.

New York Post. https://nypost.com/2020/01/23/revolting-video-shows-woman-devouring-bat-amid-coronavirus-outbreak/.

20. Huang et al., Clinical features; Zhang, T., Wu, Q., & Zhang, Z. (2020). Probable pangolin origin of SARS-CoV-2 associated with the COVID-19 outbreak. *Current Biology*, *30*(7), 1346–1351. See also Joint WHO-China Study. (2021, March 30). *WHO-convened global study of origins of SARS-CoV-2: China Part, 14 January–10 February 2021*. World Health Organization. https://www.who.int/publications/i/item/who-convened-global-study-of-origins-of-sars-cov-2-china-part.

21. Zhan, M. (2009). *Other-worldly: Making Chinese medicine through transnational frames*. Durham, NC: Duke University Press.

22. Zhan, M. (2005). Civet cats, fried grasshoppers, and David Beckham's pajamas: Unruly bodies after SARS. *American Anthropologist*, *107*(1), 31–42.

23. Li, P. (2007). Enforcing wildlife protection in China the legislative and political solutions. *China Information*, *21*(1), 71–107; Mason, K. (2016). *Infectious change: Reinventing Chinese public health after an epidemic*. Stanford, CA: Stanford University Press; Hanson, M. (2011). *Speaking of epidemics in Chinese medicine: Disease and the geographic imagination in late imperial China*. New York: Routledge, pp. 162–168.

24. Interview with *Vox*, March 6, 2020. https://www.vox.com/videos/2020/3/6/21168006/coronavirus-covid19-china-pandemic.

25. Lynteris, C. (2016). The prophetic faculty of epidemic photography: Chinese wet markets and the imagination of the next pandemic. *Visual Anthropology*, *29*(2), 118–132.

26. Wang, W., et al. (2019). Captive breeding of wildlife resources: China's revised supply-side approach to conservation. *Wildlife Society Bulletin*, *43*(3), 427.

27. Chinese Academy of Engineering (CAE). (2017). *Research report on the sustainable development strategy of China's wild animal farming and industry*. Beijing: Chinese Academy of Engineering.

28. Ibid.

29. Wang et al., Captive breeding.

30. Ibid.; Watts, J. (2004). China culls wild animals to prevent new SARS threat. *Lancet, 363*, 134.

31. Ibid.

32. Mason, *Infectious change*; Hanson, *Speaking of epidemics*, pp. 162–168.

33. Li, W., et al. (2005). Bats are natural reservoirs of SARS-like coronaviruses. *Science, 310*(5748), 676–679; Hu et al., Bat origin; Cui et al., Origin and evolution.

34. Chinese Science Communication. (2019, December 11). *Youth in the wild: Invisible defender* [video]. *The Paper.* https://www.thepaper.cn/newsDetail_forward_5200198.

35. Ibid.; Tao, P. (2017, May 3). Wuhan experts caught tens of thousands of "worms" [animal vectors] for virus research. *People.* http://hb.people.com.cn/n2/2017/0503/c192237-30124563.html; This 80s guy catches mosquitoes to inspect them, and goes into the mountains late at night to catch tens of thousands of bats [video]. (2017, May 4). *Baijiahao.* https://baijiahao.baidu.com/s?id=1566432263270047.

36. Ibid. See also Guo, W., et al., (2013). Phylogeny and origins of hantaviruses harbored by bats, insectivores, and rodents. *PLoS Pathogens, 9*(2), e1003159.

37. *Youth in the wild.*

38. Tao, Wuhan experts.

39. *Youth in the wild.*

40. Ibid.

41. Li et al., "Bats are natural reservoirs"; Cyranoski, D. (2017). Bat cave solves mystery of deadly SARS Virus, and suggests new outbreak could occur. *Nature, 552*(7683), 15–16.

42. Cui et al., Origin and evolution, p. 190, emphasis added.

43. Qiu, J. (2006). Chasing plagues. *Scientific American, 322*(6): 24–32.

44. Shi, Z. (2020, July 24). Reply to Science Magazine. *Science Magazine.*

45. Peiris, J., et al. (2003). Coronavirus as a possible cause of severe acute respiratory syndrome. *Lancet, 361*(9366), 1319–25; Poon, L., et al. (2003). Rapid diagnosis of a coronavirus associated with severe acute respiratory syndrome (SARS). *Clinical Chemistry, 49*(6): 953–955.

46. Kleinman & Watson, SARS. Kaufman, J. (2006). SARS and China's health-care response: Better to be both red and expert! In A. Kleinman & J. Watson (Eds.), *SARS in China: Prelude to pandemic?* Stanford, CA: Stanford University Press.

47. WHO. (2020, July 30). *Timeline of WHO's Response to COVID-19.* World Health Organization. https://www.who.int/emergencies/diseases/novel-coronavirus-2019/interactive-timeline.

48. Yang, Y., et al. (2015). Two mutations were critical for bat-to-human transmission of Middle East respiratory syndrome coronavirus. *Journal of Virology, 89*(17), 9119–9123; Menachery, V. D., et al. (2015). A SARS-like cluster of circulating bat coronaviruses shows potential for human emergence. *Nature Medicine, 21*(12), 1508–1513.

49. Lipsitch, M. (2018). Why do exceptionally dangerous gain-of-function experiments in influenza? In Yohei Yamauchi (Ed.), *Influenza virus: Methods and protocols* (pp. 589–608). New York: Humana Press; Kaiser, J. (2014, November 17). Moratorium on risky virology studies leaves work at 14 institutions in limbo. *Science Magazine.*

50. Weiss, S., Yitzhaki, S., & Shapira, S. (2015). Lessons to be learned from recent biosafety incidents in the United States. *Israel Medical Association Journal, 17*(5), 269–273; Klotz, L. (2019, February 25). Human error in high-biocontainment labs: A likely pandemic threat. *Bulletin of the Atomic Scientists.*

51. Ibid.

52. Ibid.

53. Byers, K. (American Biological Safety Association and Dana–Farber/Harvard Cancer Center). (2013). *LAI lessons learned and the need for an LAI reporting system.* Research paper presented at the 2nd International Biosafety and Biocontainment Symposium of the USDA ARS, February 4–7, Alexandria, Virginia, USA; Zhang, L. (2020, May 20). Coronavirus leaked from a lab? Blame capitalism, not China. *Al Jazeera.*

54. Mason, *Infectious change*; Lakoff, A. (2017). *Unprepared: Global health in a time of emergency.* Berkeley, CA: University of California Press; Elbe, S. (2018). *Pandemics, pills, and politics: Governing global health security.* Baltimore, MD: Johns Hopkins University Press.

55. Lakoff, *Unprepared,* p. 83.

56. Ibid.

57. Summers, W. (2012). *The great Manchurian plague of 1910–1911: The geopolitics of an epidemic disease.* New Haven, CT: Yale University Press; Lynteris, C. (2016). *Ethnographic plague: Configuring disease on the Chinese-Russian frontier.* New York: Springer.

58. Kleinman & Watson, SARS; Knobler, S., et al. (2004). *Learning from SARS: Preparing for the next disease outbreak.* Washington, DC: National Academies Press.

59. Ye, Y. (2010). *Biography of Zhong Nanshan.* Beijing: Writers Publishing House.

60. World Health Organization. (2003, April 7). *Update 95—SARS: Chronology of a serial killer.* https://www.who.int/csr/don/2003_07_04/en/.

61. Huang, Y. (2004). The SARS epidemic and its aftermath in China: A political perspective. In *Learning from SARS,* pp. 116–136.

62. Academician Li Lanjuan's team won the 2017 National Science and Technology Progress Special Award. (2020, Janu-

ary 12). *China News Network.* http://www.chinanews.com/sh/2018/01-12/8422134.shtml.

63. Ye, *Biography.*

64. Hanson, *Speaking of epidemics*, p. 166.

65. Ye, *Biography.* Hanson notes that "WHO officials saw [TCM] practiced when they visited the cases on April 7th, though none publicly commented on it" (*Speaking of epidemics*, p. 166).

66. Shangguan, Z., Wang, M., & Sun, W. (2020). What caused the outbreak of COVID-19 in China: From the perspective of crisis management. *International Journal of Environmental Research and Public Health*, *17*(9), 3279.

67. Mason, *Infectious change*; Mason, Divergent trust.

68. Anderson, R., et al. (2004). Epidemiology, transmission dynamics and control of SARS: The 2002–2003 epidemic. *Philosophical Transactions of the Royal Society of London. Series B: Biological Sciences*, *359*(1447), 1091–1105.

69. Naylor, C. D., Chantler, C., & Griffiths, S. (2004). Learning from SARS in Hong Kong and Toronto. *JAMA*, *291*(20), 2483–2487; Summers, *The great Manchurian plague*; Lynteris, *Ethnographic plague*; Hanson, *Speaking of epidemics.*

70. Bu, L. (2017). *Public health and the modernization of China, 1865–2015.* New York: Taylor & Francis; Yip, W., & Hsiao, W. (2014). Harnessing the privatisation of China's fragmented health-care delivery. *Lancet*, *384*(9945): 805–818.

71. Bu, *Public health.* Kaufman, SARS and China's health-care response.

72. Zhi, Y., Wilson, J., & Shen, H. (2005). SARS vaccine: Progress and challenge. *Cell and Molecular Immunology*, *2*(2), 103–104.

73. Elbe, *Pandemics.*

74. Davis, *The monster enters*, p. 10.

75. Elbe, *Pandemics.*

CHAPTER 2

1. Andersen, K., et al. (2020). The proximal origin of SARS-CoV-2. *Nature Medicine*, *26*(4), 450–452; Shang, J., et al. (2020). Structural basis of receptor recognition by SARS-CoV-2. *Nature*, *581*(7807), 221–224.

2. Huang, C., et al. (2020). Clinical features of patients infected with 2019 novel coronavirus in Wuhan, China. *Lancet*, *395*(10223), 497–506.

3. Zhang, T., Wu, Q., & Zhang, Z. (2020). Probable pangolin origin of SARS-CoV-2 associated with the COVID-19 outbreak. *Current Biology*, *30*(7); Shi, J., et al. (2020). Susceptibility of ferrets, cats, dogs, and other domesticated animals to SARS–coronavirus 2. *Science*, *368*(6494), 1016–1020.

4. This has also been shown regarding pneumonic plague in northeastern China at the turn of the twentieth century and influenza in southern China at the turn of the twenty-first century. See Lynteris, C. (2016). *Ethnographic plague: Configuring disease on the Chinese-Russian frontier.* New York: Springer; and Wallace, R. (2016). *Big farms make big flu: Dispatches on infectious disease, agribusiness, and the nature of science.* New York: Monthly Review Press.

5. Oldstone, M. (2009). *Viruses, plagues, and history: Past, present, and future.* Oxford: Oxford University Press; Snowden, F. (2019). *Epidemics and society: From the Black Death to the present.* New Haven, CT: Yale University Press.

6. Peet, R., Robbins, P., & Watts, M. (2010). *Global political ecology.* New York: Routledge; Kallis, G. (2011). In defence of degrowth. *Ecological Economics*, *70*(5), 873–880; Bello, W. (2019). *Paper dragons: China and the next great crash.* London: Zed Books.

7. Scott, J. (2010). *The art of not being governed: An anarchist history of upland Southeast Asia.* New Haven, CT: Yale University Press.

8. Zhang, L., & Qi, G. (2019). Bottom-up self-protection responses to China's food safety crisis. *Canadian Journal of Development Studies*, *40*(1), 113–130; Zhang, L. (2020). From left behind to leader: Gender, agency, and food sovereignty in China. *Agriculture and Human Values*, *37*(4), 1111–1123.

9. Chinese Academy of Engineering (CAE). (2017). *Research report on the sustainable development strategy of China's wild animal farming and industry.* Beijing: Chinese Academy of Engineering.

10. This increased demand has taken place across East Asia. Loh, C. (2004). SARS and China: Old vs. new politics. In *At the epicentre: Hong Kong and the SARS outbreak* (pp. 163–177). Hong Kong: Hong Kong University Press.

11. China is breeding huge wild rats being sold for $40 per kilo for its "nutritious meat" that can detoxify and make them prettier. (2020, April 21). *Science Times*. https://www.sciencetimes.com/articles/25404/20200421/china-breeding-huge-wild -rats-being-sold-40-per-kilo.htm

12. Ibid.; Loh, SARS and China.

13. CAE, China's wild animal farming.

14. Zhong Nanshan: The new coronavirus is likely to come from game such as bamboo rats and badgers. (2020, January 20). CCTV News Report. Archived by the author.

15. Aisher, A. (2016). Scarcity, alterity and value: Decline of the pangolin, the world's most trafficked mammal. *Conservation and Society*, *14*(4), 317–329.

16. Wu, S., et al. (2004). Assessment of threatened status of Chinese pangolin. *Chinese Journal of Applied Environmental Biology*, *10*(4): 456–461.

17. Aisher, Scarcity.

18. United Nations Environment Programme and International Livestock Research Institute (2020). *Preventing the next pandemic: Zoonotic diseases and how to break the chain of transmission.* Nairobi, Kenya: UNEP/ILRI.

19. Joint WHO-China Study. (2021, March 30). *WHO-convened global study of origins of SARS-CoV-2: China Part, 14 January–10 February 2021*. United Nations. https://www.who.int/publications/i/item/who-convened-global-study-of-origins-of-sars-cov-2-china-part, p. 9.

20. Wallace, R. (2020). *Dead epidemiologists: On the origins of COVID-19*. New York: Monthly Review Press; Joint WHO-China Study.

21. Joint WHO-China Study, p. 9.

22. Zhou, H. et al. (2021, March 8). Identification of novel bat coronavirus sheds light on the evolutionary origins of SARS-CoV-2 and related viruses. Preprint, *bioRxiv*. doi: 10.1101/2021.03.08.434390; Hul, V. et al. (2021, January 26). A novel SARS-CoV-2 related coronavirus in bats from Cambodia. Preprint, *bioRxiv*. doi: 10.1101/2021.01.26.428212; Wacharapluesadee, S., et al. (2021). Evidence for SARS-CoV-2 related coronaviruses circulating in bats and pangolins in Southeast Asia. *Nature Communications, 12*, 972.

23. Dieball, S., & Rosner, H. (2013). Geographical dimensions of mining and transport: Cases studies in mountainous Yunnan. In T. Hirzel, & N. Kim (Eds.), *Mining, monies and culture in early modern societies: East Asian and global perspectives* (pp. 241–261). Leiden: Verlag Münster.

24. Mojiang Hani Autonomous County, Annual Government Reports for 2006, 2012, and 2014.

25. All information in this paragraph derived from Li, X. (2013). *Analysis of six patients with severe pneumonia caused by unknown virus* (MA thesis, Kunming Medical University).

26. Li, W., et al. (2005). Bats are natural reservoirs of SARS-like coronaviruses. *Science, 310*(5748), 676–679

27. Li, *Analysis of six patients*, p. 57.

28. Wu, Z. et al. (2014). Novel henipa-like virus, Mojiang paramyxovirus, in rats, China, 2012. *Emerging Infectious Dis-*

eases, 20(6), 1064; Stone, R. (2014, March 20). A new killer virus in China?, *Science Magazine*. https://www.sciencemag .org/news/2014/03/new-killer-virus-china.

29. Huang, C. (2017). *Novel virus discovery in bat and the exploration of receptor bat coronavirus HKU9* (PhD dissertation, Chinese Center for Disease Control and Prevention, Beijing), p. 83.

30. Ibid., p. 83.

31. Ge, X., et al. (2013). Isolation and characterization of a bat SARS-like coronavirus that uses the ACE2 receptor. *Nature, 503*(7477), 535–538.

32. Ge, X., et al. (2016). Coexistence of multiple coronaviruses in several bat colonies in an abandoned mineshaft. *Virologica Sinica, 31*(1), 31–40.

33. Ge et al., Coexistence, which identifies it as "RaBtCoV4991 (KP876546)"; Zhou, P., et al. (2020). A pneumonia outbreak associated with a new coronavirus of probable bat origin. *Nature, 579*(7798), which identifies it as "BatCoV RaTG13"; Joint WHO-China Study, 2021.

34. Ge et al., Coexistence, p. 37.

35. Yunnan Provincial Health Commission. (2012, November 29). Notice on further strengthening the diagnosis, reporting, and disposal of cases of pneumonia of unknown origin (public notice).

36. Mojiang Hani Autonomous County. (2016, December 20). Emergency plan for group incidents caused by production safety accidents. Normative document approved by the Pu'er City Government.

37. Ge et al., Coexistence, p. 38.

38. Qiu, J. (2020, June 1). How China's "bat woman" hunted down viruses from SARS to the new coronavirus. *Scientific American*. Emphasis added. https://www.scientificamerican .com/article/how-chinas-bat-woman-hunted-down-viruses -from-sars-to-the-new-coronavirus1/.

39. Ibid.

40. Rahalkar, M., & Bahulikar, R. (2020, May 20). Understanding the origin of "BatCoVRaTG13," a virus closest to SARS-CoV-2. Preprints, 2020050322, https://www.preprints.org/manuscript/202005.0322/v2; Latham, J., & Wilson, A. (2020, July 15). A proposed origin for SARS-CoV-2 and the COVID-19 pandemic. *Independent Science News*. https://www.independentsciencenews.org/commentaries/a-proposed-origin-for-sars-cov-2-and-the-covid-19-pandemic/; Xiao, B., & Xiao, L. (2020). The possible origins of 2019-nCoV coronavirus. Preprint uploaded on February 6 and retracted by February 15 (see chapter 4).

41. Joint WHO-China Study, p. 119.

42. Zhou et al., Identification. Zhang Jinshuo is featured in the "Nature Explorer" episode filmed in 2014, broadcast on Hunan Satellite TV, April 10, 2015.

43. Zhang S., Zhang J., & Zhang L. (2008). Peculiar fake nipples on bats. *China Nature, 6*, 32–33.

44. Daszak, P. (2020, June 9). Ignore the conspiracy theories: Scientists know Covid-19 wasn't created in a lab. *The Guardian*. https://www.theguardian.com/commentisfree/2020/jun/09/conspiracies-covid-19-lab-false-pandemic.

45. Joint WHO-China Study, p. 9.

46. Ibid., p. 114.

47. Ibid., p. 116.

48. Zhang, L., et al. (2009). Conservation of bats in China: Problems and recommendations. *Fauna & Flora International, 43*(2), 180. Emphasis added.

49. Zhou et al., A pneumonia outbreak; Ge et al., Coexistence; Shang, Structural basis; Zhou et al., Identification; Joint WHO-China Study.

50. Zhang, L. (2020, May 20). Coronavirus leaked from a lab? Blame capitalism, not China. *Al Jazeera*. https://www.aljazeera.com/opinions/2020/5/20/coronavirus-leaked-from-a-lab-blame-capitalism-not-china.

51. Wang, N., et al. (2018). Serological evidence of bat SARS-related coronavirus infection in humans, China. *Virologica Sinica*, *33*(1), 104–107.

52. Wang et al., Serological evidence, p. 106.

53. Li, H., et al. (2019). Human-animal interactions and bat coronavirus spillover potential among rural residents in Southern China. *Biosafety and Health*, *1*(2), 84–90.

54. Dieball & Rossner, Geographical dimensions.

55. Wang, Y., et al. (2013). Mobile livelihoods among ethnic minorities in China: Insights from Yunnan. *Norwegian Journal of Geography*, *67*(4), 187–199.

56. Zhao, X., et al. (2020). Spatiotemporal trends of malaria in relation to economic development and cross-border movement along the China–Myanmar border in Yunnan Province. *Korean Journal of Parasitology*, *58*(3), 267.

57. Fu, W., et al. (2010). Characterizing the "fragmentation–barrier" effect of road networks on landscape connectivity: A case study in Xishuangbanna, Southwest China. *Landscape and Urban Planning*, *95*(3), 122–129; Eisenberg, J., et al. (2006). Environmental change and infectious disease: how new roads affect the transmission of diarrheal pathogens in rural Ecuador. *Proceedings of the National Academy of Sciences*, *103*(51), 19460–19465.

58. Zhang, Y., & Li, S. (2019). The current situation, problems and suggestions of e-commerce targeted poverty alleviation in Yunnan Province. *Financial Economics*, *26*(8), 17–20.

59. Zhou et al., Identification; Hul et al. A novel SARS-CoV-2; Wacharapluesadee et al., Evidence; Yang, L. (2015). Rural tourism and poverty alleviation: The case of Nujiang, Yunnan, China. *International Journal of Tourism Anthropology*, *4*(4), 343–366; World Bank. (2019). Developing nature-based tourism as a strategic sector for green growth in Lao PDR: Synthesis report. https://openknowledge.worldbank.org/handle/10986/33095?show=full.

60. Mojiang Hani Autonomous County, Annual government reports for 2006 and 2015.

61. Huang, G., Zhou, W., & Ali, S. (2011). Spatial patterns and economic contributions of mining and tourism in biodiversity hotspots: A case study in China. *Ecological Economics*, *70*(8), 1492–1498.

62. This is also Rob Wallace's leading hypothesis in *Dead Epidemiologists*.

63. Forster, P., et al. (2020). Phylogenetic network analysis of SARS-CoV-2 genomes. *Proceedings of the National Academy of Sciences*, *117*(17), 9241–9243.

64. Vidal, J. (2020, March 18). Destroyed habitat creates the perfect conditions for coronavirus to emerge. *Scientific American*/Ensia.

65. Joint WHO-China Study, p. 82.

66. Huang et al., Clinical features; Li, Q., et al. (2020). Early transmission dynamics in Wuhan, China, of novel coronavirus–infected pneumonia. *New England Journal of Medicine*, *382*, 1199–1207; WHO. (2020, January 12). Novel coronavirus—China. *WHO Disease Outbreak News*.

67. Li et al., Early transmission.

68. Shangguan, Z., Wang, M., & Sun, W. (2020). What caused the outbreak of COVID-19 in China: From the perspective of crisis management. *International Journal of Environmental Research and Public Health*, *17*(9), 3279.

69. Ren, L., et al. (2020). Identification of a novel coronavirus causing severe pneumonia in human: A descriptive study. *Chinese Medical Journal*, *133*(9), 1015–1024; Zhao J., & Huang, Y. (2020, February 26). Traceability of new coronavirus gene sequencing: When did the alarm sound? *Caixin*. Archived by the author.

70. Gao, S. (2020, February 8). She was the first to find signs of the new coronavirus pneumonia epidemic and reported sus-

picious cases as soon as possible. *Workers Daily*. Archived by the author; Fan, W., Yang, C., & Cui, M. (2020, February 6). Ringing the alarm: Wuhan doctor awarded for making first warning of novel disease before outbreak. *Global Times*. Archived by the author.

71. The 2019-nCoV Outbreak Joint Field Epidemiology Investigation Team & Li, Q. (2020). An outbreak of NCIP (2019-nCoV) infection in China—Wuhan, Hubei Province, 2019–2020. *China CDC Weekly*, *2*(5), 79–80.

72. Zhao & Huang, Traceability.

73. Wuhan Municipal Health Commission, Department of Medical Administration. (2019, December 30). Urgent notice on the treatment of pneumonia of unknown cause; Urgent notice of the Municipal Health Commission on reporting the treatment of pneumonia of unknown cause. Archived by the author.

74. Zhao & Huang, Traceability.

75. Wuhan Municipal Health Commission. (2019, December 31.). Wuhan Municipal Health Commission information bulletin about the current pneumonia epidemic situation in our city (press release). http://wjw.wuhan.gov.cn/front/web/showDetail/2019123108989.

76. Ibid.

77. Pneumonia of unknown cause found in Wuhan, Hubei National Health Commission expert team has arrived in Wuhan. (2019, December 31). *CCTV-13*. http://tv.cctv.com/2019/12/31/VIDE9N8qRty36PkLirFVxMW6191231.shtm; 27 cases of viral pneumonia reported in central China's Wuhan City. (2019, December 31). *CGTN*. https://news.cgtn.com/news/2019-12-31/Authorities-begin-testing-after-pneumonia-cases-in-central-China-MRPvtFbCve/index.html; Zuo, M., Cheng, L., Yan, A., & Yau, C. (2019, December 31). Hong Kong takes emergency measures as mystery "pneumonia" infects dozens in

China's Wuhan city. *South China Morning Post.* https://www
.scmp.com/news/china/politics/article/3044050/mystery-illness
-hits-chinas-wuhan-city-nearly-30-hospitalised.

78. WHO, Novel coronavirus; WHO. (2020, January 21).
Novel coronavirus (2019-nCoV): Situation report 1. https://www
.who.int/emergencies/diseases/novel-coronavirus-2019/situation
-reports.

CHAPTER 3

1. Guo, T. (2020, April 9). What did we do before Wuhan
was "closed"? Chang'an Avenue official WeChat account, *Beijing
Daily.* http://www.bjd.com.cn/a/202004/09/WS5e8f3d13e4b0df
866a94d2.html

2. Prashad, V., Du, X., & Zhu, W. (2020). *China and corona
shock.* Tricontinental, Institute for Social Research. https://thetri
continental.org/studies-2-coronavirus/.

3. Shangguan, Z., Wang, M., & Sun, W. (2020). What
caused the outbreak of COVID-19 in China: From the perspective of crisis management. *International Journal of Environmental Research and Public Health, 17*(9), 3279.

4. Expert review: Behind the reporting failure of "unexplained
pneumonia." (2020, March 2). *China News Weekly* official
WeChat account. Archived by the author; Zeng Guang: When
the Wuhan epidemic broke out, the expert team's voice did not
let the main leaders of the province and city hear it in time.
(2020, March 25). *Beijing Evening News* official WeChat account.
Archived by the author; Dong, X. (2020, February 1). Ma Guo-
qiang, Secretary of the Wuhan Municipal Party Committee: If I
decide earlier, the result will be better than now. CCTV interview
reported in *Sohu.* https://www.sohu.com/a/369845313_167569

5. Qin, J. et al., (2020, February 7). New coronavirus pneumonia "whistleblower" Li Wenliang: The truth is the most

important (update). *Caixin*. https://china.caixin.com/2020-02
-07/101509761.html; Gong J. (2020, March 10). Whistlegiver.
People. Archived by the author.

6. Zhao J., & Huang, Y., (2020, February 26). Traceability
of new coronavirus gene sequencing: When did the alarm
sound? *Caixin*. Archived by the author.

7. Ibid.

8. Qin J. et al., New coronavirus pneumonia "whistle-
blower"; Li, Q., et al. (2020). Early transmission dynamics in
Wuhan, China, of novel coronavirus–infected pneumonia.
New England Journal of Medicine, 382, 1199–1207.

9. Zhuang, P. (2020, February 28). Chinese laboratory that
first shared coronavirus genome with world ordered to close
for "rectification," hindering its Covid-19 research. *South China
Morning Post*. https://www.scmp.com/news/china/society/article/
3052966/chinese-laboratory-first-shared-coronavirus-genome
-world-ordered.

10. Guo, What did we do; Shangguan et al., What caused
the outbreak.

11. Shangguan et al., What caused the outbreak.

12. Ibid.

13. Expert review.

14. Ibid.; Huang, C., et al. (2020). Clinical features of patients
infected with 2019 novel coronavirus in Wuhan, China. *Lancet*,
395(10223), 497–506.

15. Chan, J., et al. (2020). A familial cluster of pneumonia
associated with the 2019 novel coronavirus indicating person-
to-person transmission: a study of a family cluster. *Lancet*,
395(10223): 514–523.

16. Expert review; Li et al., Early transmission.

17. Shangguan et al., What caused the outbreak.

18. Expert review; Guo, What did we do.

19. Li et al., Early transmission.

20. Shangguan et al., What caused the outbreak; Huang et al., Clinical features.

21. Wang, S., Zhang C., & Wu Q. (2020, January 22). Wuhan's novel pneumonia: Why hasn't it attracted more attention until today? *Sanlien Life Weekly*. https://news.sina.cn/gn/2020-01-22/detail-iihnzhha4142146.d.html

22. Gong, Whistlegiver; Hua, X. (2020, April 14). Chinese doctor recalls first encounter with mysterious virus. *Xinhua*. www.Xinhuanet.com/english/2020-04/16/c_138982435.htm

23. Expert review; Shangguang et al., What caused the outbreak.

24. Wang, C., et al. (2020). A novel coronavirus outbreak of global health concern. *Lancet*, 395, 470–473; WHO, Novel coronavirus; WHO. (2020, January 21). *Novel coronavirus (2019-nCoV): Situation report 1*. https://www.who.int/emergencies/diseases/novel-coronavirus-2019/situation-reports

25. Shangguan et al., What caused the outbreak.

26. Social media messages archived by the author.

27. Wang et al., Wuhan's novel pneumonia..

28. Shangguan et al., What caused the outbreak.

29. High-level expert group meets in Wuhan. (2020, January 19). *Beijing News*. Archived by the author; Guo, What did we do.

30. Academician Li Lanjuan's team won the 2017 National Science and Technology Progress Special Award. (2018, January 12). *China News Network*.

31. Wuhan Municipal Health Commission. (2020, January 19). Notification of Wuhan Municipal Health Commission on pneumonia caused by new coronavirus infection (press release). Archived by author.

32. Shangguan et al., What caused the outbreak.

33. Guo, What did we do.

34. Guo, What did we do; Zhong Nanshan: The new coronavirus is likely to come from game such as bamboo rats and

badgers. (2020, January 20). CCTV News Report. Archived by the author; Expert review.

35. Shangguan et al., What caused the outbreak.

36. Ibid.

37. Ibid.; triangulated with the author's digital archive.

38. Crossley, G., & Williams, A. (2020, January 23). Wuhan lockdown "unprecedented," shows commitment to contain virus: WHO representative in China. *Reuters.* https://www.reuters.com/article/us-china-health-who-idUSKBN1ZM1G9.

39. Li et al., Early transmission.

40. WHO. (2020, January 23). *Novel coronavirus (2019-nCoV): Situation report 3.* https://www.who.int/emergencies/diseases/novel-coronavirus-2019/situation-reports.

41. Ibid.

42. UN health emergency committee to re-convene on global threat posed by China coronavirus. (2020, January 22). *UN News.* https://news.un.org/en/story/2020/01/1055821.

43. You, J., Expert, P., & Costelloe, C. (2020, January 13). Using text mining to track outbreak trends in global surveillance of emerging diseases: ProMED-mail. Preprint, *medRxiv.* https://www.medRxiv.org/content/10.1101/2020.01.10.20017145v1; Chen, T., et al. (2020, January 19). A mathematical model for simulating the transmission of Wuhan novel coronavirus. Preprint, *medRxiv.* https://www.bioRxiv.org/content/10.1101/2020.01.19.911669v1.

44. WHO, *Situation report 3*; Imai, N., et al. (2020, January 22). Report 2: Estimating the potential total number of novel Coronavirus cases in Wuhan City, China. Imperial College London. https://doi.org/10.25561/77150.

45. Science is political in at least two senses: (1) all researchers have political views that are often subtly (or not so subtly) reflected in their work (for example, in the choice of topics); and (2) all science has political consequences of which the scientists themselves may be unaware (Greenhalgh, S. (2018).

Making demography astonishing: Lessons in the politics of population science. *Demography*, *55*(2), 722). See also Backhaus, T. (2019). Acknowledging that science is political is a prerequisite for science-based policy. *Integrated Environmental Assessment and Management*, *15*(3), 310–311.

46. Zhao & Huang, Traceability.

47. Terry, M. (2020, February 5). China's Wuhan Institute files to patent the use of Gilead's remdesivir for coronavirus. *BioSpace.* https://www.biospace.com/article/china-s-wuhan-institute-files-to-patent-the-use-of-gilead-s-remdesivir-for-coronavirus/.

CHAPTER 4

1. WHO. (2020, January 31). *Novel coronavirus (2019-nCoV): Situation report 11.* https://www.who.int/emergencies/diseases/novel-coronavirus-2019/situation-reports.

2. *WHO situation reports 18, 25, 32,* and *40*.

3. The significance of these declarations is discussed further in the next chapter.

4. On February 29, the Diamond Princess cruise ship, docked under quarantine in Japan, also carried 705 individuals with confirmed cases of COVID-19, six of whom had passed away. *WHO situation reports 11, 20, 30,* and *40*.

5. Fang, F. (2020). *Wuhan diary: Dispatches from a quarantined city.* San Francisco: HarperCollins, p. xii.

6. Ibid. p. 352.

7. Han, R. (2018). *Contesting cyberspace in China: Online expression and authoritarian resilience.* New York: Columbia University Press.

8. Ibid.

9. Feng, S., et al. (2020). Rational use of face masks in the COVID-19 pandemic. *Lancet, Respiratory Medicine*, *8*(5), 434–

436; Horii, M. (2014). Why do the Japanese wear masks?. *Electronic Journal of Contemporary Japanese Studies*, *14*(2), 8.

10. Fan, P., et al. (2020). Analysis of the psychology and behavior of the public during COVID-19 epidemic and its countermeasures. *Social Science Review*, *35*, 1–5; McKenna, M. (2020, February 4). Amid coronavirus fears, a mask shortage could spread globally. *Wired*. https://www.wired.com/story/amid-coronavirus-fears-a-mask-shortage-could-spread-globally; social media materials archived by the author.

11. Wang, M., et al. (2020). Mask crisis during the COVID-19 outbreak. *European Review of Medical and Pharmacological Sciences*, *24*(6), 3397–3399; McKenna, Amid coronavirus fears.

12. Fang, *Wuhan diary*; social media posts archived by the author.

13. Social media posts archived by the author.

14. Social media posts archived by the author.

15. Ding, L., et al. (2020). An interim review of lessons from the novel coronavirus (SARS-CoV-2) outbreak in China. *Scientia Sinica Vitae*, *50*, 247–257; Yip, W., & Hsiao, W. (2014). Harnessing the privatisation of China's fragmented health-care delivery. *Lancet*, *384*(9945), 805–818; Bu, L. (2017). *Public health and the modernization of China, 1865–2015*. New York: Taylor & Francis, p. 278.

16. Social media posts archived by the author.

17. Davis, M. (2020). *The monster enters: COVID-19, avian flu and the plagues of capitalism*. New York: OR Books.

18. Lai, X., et al. (2020). Coronavirus disease 2019 (COVID-2019) infection among health care workers and implications for prevention measures in a tertiary hospital in Wuhan, China. *JAMA Network Open*, *3*(5), e209666; He, Y., et al. (2020). Nosocomial infection among patients with COVID-19: A retrospective data analysis of 918 cases from a single center in Wuhan, China. *Infection Control and Hospital Epidemiology*, *41*(8), 982–983.

19. Social media posts archived by the author.

20. Bu, Public Health; Xu, J., Gorsky, M., & Mills, A. (2019). Historical roots of hospital centrism in China (1835–1949): A path dependence analysis. *Social Science and Medicine, 226,* 56–62. Kaufman, J. (2006) SARS and China's health-care response: Better to be both red and expert! In A. Kleinman & J. Watson (Eds.), *SARS in China: Prelude to pandemic?* Stanford, CA: Stanford University Press.

21. Xu, J., Gorsky, M., & Mills, A. (2020). A path dependence analysis of hospital dominance in China (1949–2018): Lessons for primary care strengthening. *Health Policy and Planning, 35*(2), 167–179. Kaufman, SARS and China's health-care response.

22. Oliveira, S. (2010). *Análise Bioética das Ações de Prevenção e Controle das Infecções Hospitalares* (Bioethical Analysis of the Actions for Prevention and Control of Hospital Infections). MA thesis, University of Brasilia.

23. Zhou, C. (2020, February 7). Coronavirus: Whistleblower Dr Li Wenliang confirmed dead of the disease at 34, after hours of chaotic messaging from hospital. *South China Morning Post.* https://www.scmp.com/news/china/society/article/3049411/coronavirus-li-wenliang-doctor-who-alerted-authorities-outbreak.

24. Deng, C., & Chin, J. (2020, February 7). Chinese doctor who issued early warning on virus dies. *Wall Street Journal.* https://www.wsj.com/articles/chinese-doctor-who-issued-early-warning-on-virus-dies-11581019816.

25. Ma, J., & Mai, J. (2020, February 7). Death of coronavirus doctor Li Wenliang becomes catalyst for "freedom of speech" demands in China. *South China Morning Post.* https://www.scmp.com/news/china/politics/article/3049606/coronavirus-doctors-death-becomes-catalyst-freedom-speech.

26. Hubei Provincial Party Committee's main responsible comrade's job adjustment, Ying Yong serves as Hubei Provin-

cial Party Committee Secretary. (2020, February 13). *Xinhua News.* http://www.Xinhuanet.com/politics/2020-02/13/c_1125568253 .htm; Tang Zhihong, director of the Huanggang Municipal Health Commission, was nominated and dismissed: Facing the inspection team questions, she did not know a thing. (2020, January 30). *The Paper.* https://www.thepaper.cn/newsDetail_ forward_5687687; During the epidemic, Wuhan has accounted for 654 people and 10 officials at the bureau level. (2020, March 2). *Jiemian.* Official WeChat account of the Political and Law Committee of the Central Committee of the Communist Party of China (Chang'an Jian). https://www.jiemian.com/article/ 4051360_foxit.html.

27. CCTV Interview with Wuhan Mayor, Zhou Xianwang. (2020, January 27). *CCTV.* https://haokan.baidu.com/v?pd=w isenatural&vid=12522697294303116134.

28. Shangguan, Z., Wang, M., & Sun, W. (2020). What caused the outbreak of COVID-19 in China: From the perspective of crisis management. *International Journal of Environmental Research and Public Health, 17*(9), 3279.

29. Li, Q., et al. (2020). Early transmission dynamics in Wuhan, China, of novel coronavirus–infected pneumonia. *New England Journal of Medicine, 382,* 1199–1207; Wang, C., et al. (2020). A novel coronavirus outbreak of global health concern. *Lancet, 395,* 470–473.

30. Zhao, S., et al. (2020). Preliminary estimation of the basic reproduction number of novel coronavirus (2019-nCoV) in China, from 2019 to 2020: A data-driven analysis in the early phase of the outbreak. *International Journal of Infectious Diseases, 92,* 214–217; Chan, J., et al. (2020). A familial cluster of pneumonia associated with the 2019 novel coronavirus indicating person-to-person transmission: a study of a family cluster. *Lancet, 395*(10223): 514–523.

31. This results from the post-SARS imperative of professionalizing public health in China according to "international

standards." Mason, K. (2016). *Infectious change: Reinventing Chinese public health after an epidemic.* Stanford, CA: Stanford University Press.

32. Ministry of Science and Technology: Publish your papers in the motherland! (2020, January 30). *Sohu.* https://www.sohu.com/a/369721616_120059213/

33. For an academic framework to the study of such phenomena, see Kapferer, J. (2013). *Rumors: Uses, interpretations, and images.* New York: Transaction Publishers.

34. Pradhan, P., et al. (2020). Uncanny similarity of unique inserts in the 2019-nCoV spike protein to HIV-1 gp120 and Gag. Preprint uploaded to *bioRxiv* January 31, 2020, withdrawn on February 2, 2020. https://www.*bioRxiv*.org/content/10.1101/2020.01.30.927871v2

35. Xiao, B., & Xiao, L. (2020). The possible origins of 2019-nCoV coronavirus. Preprint uploaded to *ResearchGate* on February 6, 2020, retracted by February 15, 2020. Archived by the author.

36. Ibid. p. 2, citing Menachery, V. D., et al. (2015). A SARS-like cluster of circulating bat coronaviruses shows potential for human emergence. *Nature Medicine, 21*(12), 1508–1513. See also Yang, Y., et al. (2015). Two mutations were critical for bat-to-human transmission of Middle East respiratory syndrome coronavirus. *Journal of Virology, 89*(17), 9119–9123.

37. Xiao & Xiao, The possible origins, p. 3.

38. Social media posts archived by the author.

39. News articles and social media posts archived by the author.

40. Stevenson, A. (2020, February 17). Senator Tom Cotton repeats fringe theory of coronavirus origins. *New York Times.* https://www.nytimes.com/2020/02/17/business/media/coronavirus-tom-cotton-china.html

41. Rao Yi wrote to Shu Hongbing, suggesting that his wife (Wang Yanyi) resign on their own initiative? (2020, February 4).

Freescience. https://t.cj.sina.com.cn/articles/view/6468995530/1 819509ca01900lv0e.

42. Yang, Z. (2020, February 17). Researcher denies rumors on novel coronavirus outbreak. *China Daily*. https://www.china daily.com.cn/a/202002/17/WS5e4a8a76a310128217278299.html; Chen Quanjiao, the real-name reporting director of Wuhan Institute of Virology? The truth is chilling. (2020, March 13). *Global Times*. http://www.81.cn/2020zt/2020-03/13/content_9767570.htm

43. Luo, Y. (2020, February 14). Xi Jinping: Incorporate biosafety into the national security system and promote the introduction of a biosafety law as soon as possible. *CCTV*. https://www.yicai.com/news/100505860.html.

44. Wu, X. (2020, January 31). The army expert group goes deep into the epidemic area to conduct scientific research. *Ministry of National Defense Network*. http://www.81.cn/jfjbmap/ content/2020-01/31/content_253028.htm; Qian, W. (2020, February 19). Major General Chen Wei, an expert on China's biological and chemical weapons epidemic prevention, takes over Wuhan P4 laboratory. *Sina Weibo*. https://weibo.com/ ttarticle/p/show?id=2309404479879126057212

45. Andersen, K., et al. (2020). The proximal origin of SARS-CoV-2. *Nature Medicine*, *26*(4), 450–452; Joint WHO-China Study. (2021, March 30). *WHO-convened global study of origins of SARS-CoV-2: China Part, 14 January–10 February 2021*. World Health Organization. https://www.who.int/publications/i/item/who -convened-global-study-of-origins-of-sars-cov-2-china-part, p. 9.

46. See chapter 2.

47. Ministry of Science and Technology, State Council, and NHC. (2020, March 3). Notice of the General Office of the National Health Commission on regulating the information release management of scientific research results of COVID-19. Archived by the author.

48. Lakoff, A. *Unprepared: Global health in a time of emergency*. Berkeley, CA: University of California Press, 2017.

49. Huoshenshan and Leishengshan Hospital's construction live stream, 40 million netizens witness the Chinese speed to combat the epidemic. (2020, January 30). State-Owned Assets Supervision and Administration Commission of the State Council (SASAC) press release. http://www.sasac.gov.cn/n2588025/n2588119/c13669614/content.html.

50. From nationwide aid to the orderly withdrawal of the medical team in Hubei. (2020, March 17). Central Commission for Discipline Inspection and State Supervision. http://www.ccdi.gov.cn/toutiao/202003/t20200317_213671.html.

51. For an in depth account of the use of TCM in the treatment of COVID-19 in China, see Ochs, S., & Garran, T. A. (2020). *Chinese medicine and COVID-19: Results and reflections from China*. Passiflora Press. On the industrialization and commodification of TCM see Zheng, Y. (2019, August 12). A healthy way of nursing the world. *China Daily*.

52. 35 days for a Wuhan patient: One day, he coughed so much that everyone was coughing when he went to the hospital. (2020, February 26). *Pengpai News*. https://www.sohu.com/a/375919216_260616.

53. Xi Jinping: Speech when inspecting the prevention and control of the new coronavirus pneumonia epidemic in Hubei Province. (2020, March 31). *Xinhua*. http://www.Xinhuanet.com/politics/leaders/2020-03/31/c_1125794013.htm.

54. Xi signs order to award 4 persons for outstanding contribution in COVID-19 fight. (2020, August 11). *Xinhua*. http://www.Xinhuanet.com/english/2020-08/11/c_139282926.htm.

CHAPTER 5

1. WHO. (2020, March 7). *Novel coronavirus (2019-nCoV): Situation report 47*. https://www.who.int/emergencies/diseases/novel-coronavirus-2019/situation-reports.

2. *WHO situation report 59* (2020, March 19).

3. Ibid., p. 1.

4. *WHO situation report 71* (2020, March 31).

5. Desheng, C. (2020, April 8). Wuhan reopens after 76-day lockdown. *China Daily*. https://global.chinadaily.com.cn/a/202004/08/WS5e8d06fc310eaeeed5099e.html; Kwok, C., & Tsang, Y. (2020, April 27). Wuhan declares "victory" as central Chinese city's last Covid-19 patients leave hospital. *South China Morning Post*. https://www.scmp.com/video/coronavirus/3081785/wuhan-declares-victory-central-chinese-citys-last-covid-19-patients-leave.

6. *WHO situation report 101* (2020, April 30).

7. Archived by author.

8. Lynch, C., & Gramer, R. (2020, March 11). US and China turn coronavirus into a geopolitical football. *Foreign Policy*. https://foreignpolicy.com/2020/03/11/coronavirus-geopolitics-china-united-states-trump-administration-competing-global-health-response/.

9. Ibid.

10. This was covered widely in US media on February 27, 2020, for example, Armour, S., & Andrews, N. (2020, February 27). Whistleblower says federal employees flown from coronavirus sites didn't follow safety protocols. *Wall Street Journal*. https://www.wsj.com/articles/whistleblower-says-federal-employees-flown-from-coronavirus-sites-didnt-follow-safety-protocols-11582840144. On March 10, the US Congress sent a letter seeking further information about the case "after receiving an inadequate reply from the Trump Administration" (Neal, R. (2020, March 10). Ways and Means leaders seek additional information from HHS regarding whistleblower allegation (press release). https://waysandmeans.house.gov/media-center/press-releases/ways-and-means-leaders-seek-additional-information-hhs-regarding). The committee took no action,

and the issue was not covered at any greater length in US media until the US Government Accountability Office released a report confirming the whistleblower's claims over a year later, on April 19, 2021 (USGAO. (2021). COVID-19: HHS should clarify agency roles for emergency return of U.S. citizens during a pandemic. Report to Congressional Addressees. GAO-21-334. https://www.gao.gov/assets/gao-21-334.pdf; Weiland, N. (2021). Health agencies compromised safety of evacuees and staff early in pandemic, watchdog says. (April 19, 2021). *New York Times*. https://www.nytimes.com/2021/04/19/us/politics/coronavirus-evacuation-gao-report.html).

11. Shear, M., et al. (2020, March 28). The lost month: How a failure to test blinded the US to COVID-19. *New York Times.* https://www.nytimes.com/2020/03/28/us/testing-coronavirus-pandemic.html; Bump, P. (2020, March 7). Which is Trump more worried about: Coronavirus numbers or coronavirus patients? *Washington Post*. https://www.washingtonpost.com/politics/2020/03/07/which-is-trump-more-worried-about-coronavirus-numbers-or-coronavirus-patients/.

12. WeChat and Weibo posts archived by the author, March 4, March 26, and May 7.

13. @realDonaldTrump, Twitter, January 24, 2020, 1:18 p.m. Archived by the author.

14. Serwer, A. (2020, March 24). Trump is inciting a coronavirus culture war to save himself. *The Atlantic*. https://www.theatlantic.com/ideas/archive/2020/03/trump-is-the-chinese-governments-most-useful-idiot/608638/.

15. Serwer, Trump is inciting; Shepherd, K. (2020, March 20). John Cornyn criticized Chinese for eating snakes. He forgot about the rattlesnake roundups back in Texas. *Washington Post*. https://www.washingtonpost.com/nation/2020/03/19/coronavirus-china-cornyn-blame/; Borger, J. (2020, April 14). US military chief: "Weight of evidence" that Covid-19 did not

originate in a lab. *The Guardian*. https://www.theguardian.com/world/2020/apr/14/covid-19-origin-lab-general-mark-milley.

16. @zlj517, Twitter, March 12, 2020, 7:37 a.m.

17. Leng, S. (2020, March 15). US urged to explain military lab shutdown. *Global Times*. https://www.globaltimes.cn/content/1182694.shtml; social media posts archived by the author.

18. Social media posts archived by the author.

19. WHO. (2020, July 30). *Timeline of WHO's Response to COVID-19*. World Health Organization. https://www.who.int/emergencies/diseases/novel-coronavirus-2019/interactive-time line, events 24 and 42.

20. Lakoff, A. *Unprepared: Global health in a time of emergency*. Berkeley, CA: University of California Press, 2017, p. 159.

21. WHO. (2020 January 30). *Statement on the second meeting of the International Health Regulations (2005) Emergency Committee regarding the outbreak of novel coronavirus (2019-nCoV)*. Geneva: WHO. https://www.who.int/news-room/detail/30-01-2020-statement-on-the-second-meeting-of-the-international-health-regulations-(2005)-emergency-committee-regarding-the-outbreak-of-novel-coronavirus-(2019-ncov).

22. WHO, *Timeline: WHO's COVID-19 response*, events 50, 57 and 63.

23. Official United Nations WeChat account. (2020, March 4). Novel coronavirus epidemic sweeps the world, WHO calls for learning from China's experience. Archived by the author.

24. Ibid.

25. McNeil, D. (2020, March 4). Inside China's all-out war on the coronavirus. *New York Times*. https://www.nytimes.com/2020/03/04/health/coronavirus-china-aylward.html.

26. Ibid.

27. Ibid.

28. Kelly, H. (2011). The classical definition of a pandemic is not elusive. *Bulletin of the World Health Organization*, *89*, 540–541.

29. Associated Press. (2020, March 9). The coronavirus outbreak sure looks like a pandemic, except to the World Health Organization. *Los Angeles Times.* https://www.latimes.com/science/story/2020-03-09/world-health-organization-resists-calling-coronavirus-outbreak-a-pandemic.

30. Kelly, The classical definition.

31. Lynch & Gramer, US and China.

32. Aslam, N. (2020, 12 March). The bear market is here! Fastest plunge of 20% on record. *Forbes.* https://www.forbes.com/sites/naeemaslam/2020/03/12/the-bear-market-is-here-fastest-plunge-of-20-on-record/#292762a6627f.

33. Xi Jinping: Speech when inspecting the prevention and control of the new coronavirus pneumonia epidemic in Hubei Province. (2020, March 31). *Xinhua.* http://www.Xinhuanet.com/politics/leaders/2020-03/31/c_1125794013.htm.

34. Speech by Xi Jinping at the opening ceremony of the 73rd World Health Assembly video conference. (2020, May 18). *Xinhua.* http://www.Xinhuanet.com/politics/leaders/2020-05/18/c_1126001593.htm.

35. Ochs, S., & Garran, T. A. (2020). *Chinese medicine and COVID-19: Results and reflections from China.* Passiflora Press; Tilley, H. (2020, May 25). How to make sense of "traditional (Chinese) medicine" in a time of covid-19: cold war origin stories and the WHO's role in making space for polyglot therapeutics. *Somatosphere.*

36. Leng, S. (2021, February 8). China provides vaccine aid to 53 developing countries, exports to 22. *Global Times.*

37. Lynch & Gramer, US and China.

38. *Global Times* official WeChat account, March 11, 2020. https://mp.weixin.qq.com/s/5JB8PT_59QnJobZAm2a1Tw.

39. There are variations in the way QR health codes are used and enforced across various cities and provinces. For more information see Hu, M. (2020, March 2). Beijing rolls out

colour-coded QR system for coronavirus tracking despite concerns over privacy, inaccurate ratings. *South China Morning Post*. https://www.scmp.com/tech/apps-social/article/3064574/beijing-rolls-out-colour-coded-qr-system-coronavirus-tracking; Huang, O. (2021). *The great debate of the digital age: Liberty, security, and COVID-19*. MA thesis, University of California, Irvine.

40. Ibid.

41. National Bureau of Statistics of China. (2021, April 16). National economy made a good start in the first quarter (press release). http://www.stats.gov.cn/english/PressRelease/202104/t20210416_1816315.html.

42. Due to epidemic, the first wave of foreign trade closures is coming! 54 million people face unemployment. (2020, March 31). *Sina Finance*. https://cj.sina.com.cn/articles/view/6241116541/173ffe17d001000kv6.

43. Li, R., et al. (2020). Substantial undocumented infection facilitates the rapid dissemination of novel coronavirus (SARS-CoV-2). *Science*, *368*(6490), 489–493.

44. Tsang, T., et al. (2020). Effect of changing case definitions for COVID-19 on the epidemic curve and transmission parameters in mainland China: a modelling study. *Lancet Public Health*, *5*(5), e289–e296.

45. Hao, X., et al. (2020). Reconstruction of the full transmission dynamics of COVID-19 in Wuhan. *Nature*, *584*, 420–424.

46. Wuhan City Government official WeChat account. (2020, August 17). Today Hubei signed 30 major projects!. Archived by author.

47. Wuhan City Government official WeChat account, archived by the author.

48. Tilley, How to make sense.

49. Prospective Industry Research Institute. (2021, February 18). Analysis of the development of the delivery sector in China

in 2020 and future trends. *Sohu*. https://www.sohu.com/a/451485686_473133.

50. National Bureau of Statistics of China. (2021, April 16). National economy; Strong start to 2021, China economy powers ahead for high-quality growth. *Xinhua*. http://www.Xinhuanet.com/english/2021-04/16/c_139884491.htm.

CHAPTER 6

1. Beijing seals off wholesale markets after coronavirus detected on fishmonger's cutting board. (2020, June 13). *Global Times*. Archived by author.

2. Ibid.

3. WHO. (2020, June 18). *Novel coronavirus (2019-nCoV): Situation report 150*. https://www.who.int/emergencies/diseases/novel-coronavirus-2019/situation-reports.

4. Ibid.

5. Morens, D., et al. (2020). The origin of COVID-19 and why it matters. *American Journal of Tropical Medicine and Hygiene, 103*(3), 958.

6. Ibid., p. 959.

7. Li, W., et al. (2005). Bats are natural reservoirs of SARS-like coronaviruses. *Science, 310*(5748), 676–679; Hu, B., Ge, X., Wang, L., & Shi, Z. (2015). Bat origin of human coronaviruses. *Virology Journal, 12*, 221; Cui, J., Li, F., & Shi, Z. (2019). Origin and evolution of pathogenic coronaviruses. *Nature Reviews Microbiology, 17*(3), 181–192; Menachery, V. D., et al. (2015). A SARS-like cluster of circulating bat coronaviruses shows potential for human emergence. *Nature Medicine, 21*(12), 1508–1513; Li, H., et al. (2019). Human-animal interactions and bat coronavirus spillover potential among rural residents in Southern China. *Biosafety and Health, 1*(2), 84–90; Fan, Y., et al. (2019). Bat coronaviruses in China. *Viruses, 11*(3), 210.

8. Morens et al., The origin, p. 958.

9. Lakoff, A. *Unprepared: Global health in a time of emergency*. Berkeley, CA: University of California Press, 2017, p. 12.

10. Rogaski, R. (2004). *Hygienic modernity: Meanings of health and disease in treaty-port China*. Berkeley, CA: University of California Press, pp. 2–3. See also Lynteris, C. (2016). *Ethnographic plague: Configuring disease on the Chinese-Russian frontier*. New York: Springer.

11. Ibid.

12. Schmalzer, S. (2016). *Red revolution, green revolution: Scientific farming in socialist China*. Chicago: University of Chicago Press.; Gross, M. (2016). *Farewell to the god of plague: Chairman Mao's campaign to deworm China*. Berkeley, CA: University of California Press; Brazelton, M. (2019). *Mass vaccination: Citizens' bodies and state power in modern China*. Syracuse, NY: Cornell University Press.

13. Tilley, H. (2020, May 25). How to make sense of "traditional (Chinese) medicine" in a time of COVID-19: Cold war origin stories and the WHO's role in making space for polyglot therapeutics. *Somatosphere*. http://somatosphere.net/2020/tcm-covid-19.html/.

14. Wang., W., et al. (2019). Captive breeding of wildlife resources: China's revised supply-side approach to conservation. *Wildlife Society Bulletin, 43*(3), 431.

15. Wang, L. (2020, April 2). From Hendra to Wuhan: Emerging bat-borne viruses in a quarter of century [video]. LabRoots, Coronavirus Virtual Event Series. https://www.labroots.com/webinar/hendra-wuhan-emerging-bat-borne-viruses-quarter-century

16. Ibid., emphasis added.

17. For the most critical strains of this literature, see Wallace, R. (2016). *Big farms make big flu: Dispatches on infectious disease, agribusiness, and the nature of science.* New York: Monthly

Review Press; Wallace, R. (2020). *Dead epidemiologists: On the origins of COVID-19.* New York: Monthly Review Press; Davis, M. (2006). *The monster at the door: The global threat of avian flu.* New York: Macmillan; Davis, M. (2020). *The monster enters: COVID-19, avian flu and the plagues of capitalism.* New York: OR Books; Blanchette, A. (2020). *Porkopolis: American animality, standardized life, and the factory farm.* Durham, NC: Duke University Press.

18. International Assessment of Agricultural Knowledge, Science and Technology for Development (IAASTD). (2009). *Agriculture at a crossroads.* Washington, DC: Island Press. More information on the IAASTD at https://wedocs.unep.org/handle/20.500.11822/8590.

19. United Nations Environment Programme and International Livestock Research Institute. (2020). *Preventing the next pandemic: Zoonotic diseases and how to break the chain of transmission.* Nairobi, Kenya: UNEP/ILRI.

20. Ibid., p. 31

21. Ibid., pp. 15, 25, 33.

22. Ibid. p. 16.

23. World Bank. (2020, June 18). China: New project to reduce risks of emerging infectious diseases through a multisectoral approach (press release number 2020/227/EAP), pp. 7, 10.

24. World Bank (2020, June 1). Emerging Infectious Diseases Prevention, Preparedness and Response Project (P173746), report number PIDA28944.

25. UNEP/ILRI, *Preventing the next pandemic*, pp. 16, 26.

26. Ibid., pp. 26–27. See also Zhang, L., & Qi, G. (2019). Bottom-up self-protection responses to China's food safety crisis. *Canadian Journal of Development Studies, 40*(1), 113–130; Zhang, L. (2020). From left behind to leader: Gender, agency, and food sovereignty in China. *Agriculture and Human Values, 37*(4), 1111–1123.

27. Baumgaertner, E., & Rainey, J. (2020, April 2). Trump administration ended pandemic early-warning program to detect coronaviruses. *Los Angeles Times*. https://www.latimes.com/science/story/2020-04-02/coronavirus-trump-pandemic-program-viruses-detection.

28. Wang, S., Zhang C., & Wu Q. (2020, January 22). Wuhan's novel pneumonia: Why hasn't it attracted more attention until today? *Sanlien Life Weekly*. https://news.sina.cn/gn/2020-01-22/detail-iihnzhha4142146.d.html.

29. Lipsitch, M. (2018). Why do exceptionally dangerous gain-of-function experiments in influenza? In Yohei Yamauchi (Ed.), *Influenza virus: Methods and protocols* (pp. 589–608). New York: Humana Press.

30. Biosafety law legislation speeds up, experts suggest strengthening laboratory management. (2020, February 25). *Beijing News*. www.bjnews.com.cn/news/2020/02/25/694826.html.

31. Lakoff, *Unprepared*.

32. Tilley, How to make sense; Huang, N. (2012). Control medical and profit-driven behavior to promote the healthy development of Chinese medicine. *Asia-Pacific Traditional Medicine*, *8*(11), 4–6.

33. Ochs, S., & Garran, T. A. (2020). *Chinese medicine and COVID-19: Results and reflections from China*. Passiflora Press.; Loh, C. (2004). SARS and China: Old vs. new politics. In *At the epicentre: Hong Kong and the SARS outbreak* (pp. 163–177). Hong Kong: Hong Kong University Press; Hanson, M. (2011). *Speaking of epidemics in Chinese medicine: Disease and the geographic imagination in late imperial China*. New York: Routledge.

34. Zheng, Y. (2019, August 12). A healthy way of nursing the world. *China Daily*. https://www.chinadaily.com.cn/a/201908/12/WS5d50a0b6a310cf3e35565167.html.

EPILOGUE

1. Hanson, M. (2020). From "Sick Man of Asia" to Sick Uncle Sam. *Current History*, *119*(817), 241–244; Rogaski, R. (2021). The Manchurian plague and COVID-19: China, the United States, and the "Sick Man," then and now. *American Journal of Public Health*, *111*(3), 423–429.

2. Joint WHO-China Study. (2021, March 30). *WHO-convened global study of origins of SARS-CoV-2: China Part, 14 January–10 February 2021*. World Health Organization. https://www.who.int/publications/i/item/who-convened-global-study-of-origins-of-sars-cov-2-china-part, p. 9.

3. Hul, V., et al. (2021, January 26). A novel SARS-CoV-2 related coronavirus in bats from Cambodia. Preprint, *bioRxiv*. doi: 10.1101/2021.01.26.428212; Wacharapluesadee, S., et al. (2021). Evidence for SARS-CoV-2 related coronaviruses circulating in bats and pangolins in Southeast Asia. *Nature Communications*, *12*, 972.

4. Joint WHO-China Study, p. 9.

5. Ibid., p. 116.

6. Editorial Board. (2020, February 28). The era of vaccine diplomacy is here. *New York Times*. https://www.nytimes.com/2021/02/28/opinion/covid-vaccine-global.html.

7. Sabino, E., et al. (2021). Resurgence of COVID-19 in Manaus, Brazil, despite high seroprevalence. *Lancet*, *397*(10273), 452–455; Cohen, J. (2021, February 8). South Africa suspends use of AstraZeneca's COVID-19 vaccine after it fails to clearly stop virus variant. *Science Magazine*. https://www.sciencemag.org/news/2021/02/south-africa-suspends-use-astrazenecas-covid-19-vaccine-after-it-fails-clearly-stop; Collier, D., et al. (2021). Sensitivity of SARS-CoV-2 B.1.1.7 to mRNA vaccine-elicited antibodies. *Nature*, *593*(7857), 136–141; Madhi, S., et al. (2021). Efficacy of the ChAdOx1 nCoV-19 Covid-19 vaccine against the B. 1.351 variant. *New England Journal of Medicine*.

DOI: 10.1056/NEJMoa2102214; Ferreira, I., et al. (2021). SARS-CoV-2 B. 1.617 emergence and sensitivity to vaccine-elicited antibodies. *bioRxiv*. https://www.bioRxiv.org/content/10.1101/2021.05.08.443253v1; Hoffmann, M., et. al. (2021). SARS-CoV-2 variant B. 1.617 is resistant to Bamlanivimab and evades antibodies induced by infection and vaccination. *bioRxiv*. https://www.bioRxiv.org/content/10.1101/2021.05.04.442663v1; Kustin, T., et al. (2021). Evidence for increased breakthrough rates of SARS-CoV-2 variants of concern in BNT162b2 mRNA vaccinated individuals. *MedRxiv*. https://www.medRxiv.org/content/10.1101/2021.04.06.21254882v1.